THE AMAZING LIFE STORY OF
EDITH BAKER
MEDIUM/HEALER

TOM BOYLE

authorHOUSE®

AuthorHouse™
1663 Liberty Drive
Bloomington, IN 47403
www.authorhouse.com
Phone: 1-800-839-8640

Published by AuthorHouse   12/05/2012

ISBN: 978-1-4772-4751-8 (sc)
ISBN: 978-1-4772-4752-5 (e)

contents

INTRODUCTION

Edith Baker and her husband Ted were mediums/healers in Bristol and the surrounding area for over fifty years. Bringing comfort to the bereaved, and many fantastic cures to the sick and disabled.

They at one time had three nursing homes in Bristol and there was always a waiting list of people wanting places, such was their reputation.

In January 1977 they went to Spain looking for a home in the sun, and in June 1997 they moved to their new home, just outside Torrevieja, on the Costa Blanca.

Any thought of retiring in the sun was soon forgotten as they found themselves involved with healing in their new house, and taking services in local churches. They purchased a plot of land with the intention of building a church adjacent to their house. Sadly Ted passed to Spirit with a massive brain haemorrhage on December 4th 1977.

Although Edith was 75 years of age, and despite the wishes of her family, she refused to go back to England. She had the church built, The Baker Foundation, and ran it very successfully.

Now in her 91st year she is still very active in the church, running two circles on a Tuesday, healing on Thursdays and after service on Sunday.

She not only attends every Sunday service, she step in to take the service if the need arises.

Mediums come from all over the U.K. to spend a week working at the Baker Foundation and return many times.

Edith Baker is a real inspiration to all who have the good to know her.

Ted and Edith Baker

Who founded the Baker Foundation in 1998

This church is filled with love and compassion. It has been said many times, the love just clings to the walls.

A warm and friendly greeting awaits you. So come and blend yourself with a haven here in Playa Flamenca.

The minute you enter the door you can feel the love and peace.

I also find a warm greeting is extended to everyone no matter who you are and especially if you are a newcomer.

Linda Buchanan

chapter 1

IN THE BEGINNING

I was born in 1922, in a cottage 250yds from the river Avon, at St Anns,

Bristol. The eldest of three children, 2 girls and 1 boy. My parents Charles and Edith, owned the boat station and Beeses tea gardens, which was a well known beauty spot in the Bristol area.

Virtually as soon as we could walk, we were encouraged to work in the business.

Which meant that every Whitsun, Easter and August bank holiday, there was no chance of going anywhere. We were all required to do whatever, ie work in the shop, taking the ferry boat over and bringing customers back, at 1 penny a time. This was when there were 12 pennies to the shilling and 240 pennies to the pound. In those days a penny was a much larger and heavier coin than it is today. Because I was quite small and could not collect the money easily, we used to put a bucket on the steps and as the passengers came off the ferry boat, they would throw the pennies in the bucket. This meant at the end of the day, usually about nine o'clock, there was quite a heavy bucket load of pennies to be carried up to the house and counted into piles of 12.

When I left school, my Mother was disappointed that instead of working in the family business, I wanted to go and work in the real world. I wanted to get a job at WD&HO Wills's tobacco factory, they had three factories in Bristol, two making cigarettes and one making cigars. In those days you could only get a job with them if you had a relative that had worked there and they had a good work record. So I said to my Father "You know Billy Wills don't you" he said "yes I know Billy" so I said "well see if you can try and do something for me". At that time my Father was coach to the area rowing club, and the directors from Wills's used to train on the Avon, at the boat house just below Beeses tea gardens, so Father was quite friendly with them and he mentioned to Billy Wills that I wanted a job with them. Billy said "well let me know when she's coming in and i'll see if I can arrange something".

Needless to say that when I went for the interview, I was told that I had got the job.

In those days we were starting work at 7am, which meant getting up at 5.30 am, walk up through the field, walk about 4 miles to get the bus into the centre of Bristol, then walk along Coronation Road to the factory. We would finish at five o'clock and then retrace our steps home. This was my routine for quite a few years. Also in those days we worked on a Saturday morning.

Because I was such a rebel and having to work Whitsun, Easter and August bank holidays in the business, I used to tell the girls at work that I had met fellow or that fellow, and we had been here or there and done this and that.

I would have the table of twenty four girls in absolute raptures, it was hilarious.

Phoebe Meredith, who was our fore woman hated my guts, and tried so many times to get me the sack, but she didn't know who it was that got me the job. There was no way she could get me out, so the next move whenever she got the opportunity was to punish me. We were supposed to strip 80 pound of leaf per day, and I was always short of my quota. But on a Saturday morning the girls would strip their leaf and pass it down the table to me. So on a Saturday, by some miracle, I always ended up over my quota, which was a mystery to Phoebe.

However she decided that she would really punish me, and so she sent me to work in the canteen. This turned out to be the best thing she could possibly have done for me. While there I learned how many slices of bread there were to a thick loaf, how many slices their were to a thin sliced loaf, and how much butter I needed for how many sandwiches, how much milk for so many cups of tea etc. At the time it didn't mean anything to me but later in life it was invaluable, as you will see later on.

One day when I was sent down to the canteen they were fully staffed and there was no place for me, so they had to find me a different job. They put me to dusting the doctors surgeries (Wills's had their own in-house doctors and dentists and opticians) this day I was dusting Dr Meadows surgery when a patient turned up, I said to the doctor," shall I leave"," no, no my dear you carry on, it's all right" he replied. So George came in," good morning George" said the doctor," how are you this morning"." I am no better. no better at all" George replied. Dr Meadows looked at him and said" George, I've told you before, until you've had your teeth out, you will never be any different". So George promptly took his false teeth out and put them on the doctor's desk. How I refrained from bursting out laughing I don't know.

I must say that medical care at Wills's was very good. At one time I was suffering from recurring mouth ulcers and they sent me to a top Harley St specialist, who burned them all out. He said "you'll never suffer from ulcers again".

"Thank god for that" I said. And the next month I had mouth ulcers. But that's another story.

Just before the outbreak of war, Ted and his friend used to come to Beeses on a Saturday morning and pith their tent in the corner of the woods, where there was a waterfall and spring. This was the only source of fresh water, and we had to pump it up to the house. This would mean pumping away for two or three hours a day.

Ted used to pay one shilling for the privilege of camping at Beeses for the weekend. My father became quite fascinated with Ted who was a great keep fit fanatic, and was also training as a boxer, which my Father was very aufait with, as he was a flyweight champion. They got on very well, until one day I went down to the tent to see what the boy's were doing. They were trying to fry eggs and bacon on a primus stove. Me being me, I took over, which was a big mistake, because from then on my Father cut off all contact with Ted. He thought it was dreadful that his daughter was getting involved with this boy.

Ted was a Saturday sailor,(like the territorial army, but with the navy) which meant that every year he did fourteen days at sea with the Royal navy. When war broke out he was at sea doing his two week training, when a telegram arrived at his home telling him to report to the Flying Fox in Bristol, this was their H.Q., but of course he was already at sea. The navy then sent the military police for him, "what are you talking about" his Mother said,

"He's already gone, he's on HMS Coventry doing his training".

So they accepted that and went away. Later on they returned for his equipment, "his equipment" said his Mother, "what equipment", "his bugle" they replied. His mother looked at them and said "young man, they need guns, not bugles.

By the time Ted came back from his two weeks at sea all this had happened, so he reported to the Flying Fox H.Q, only to discover that the day before, all his mates had been sent to

Devonport to pick up a ship. Now he was the only Bristolian, on his own.

Ted in his working life, worked for Mardon Son and Hall, the company that made the packaging for Wills's cigarettes, so he was making the packets for my cigarettes.

Ted went off to war, it was at that time we discovered that we had a great link between us. I always sensed where he was and what he was doing, and he always knew where I was and what I was doing, which was a bit awkward at times, because being slim, blond and in those days quite dishy, he started to worry that by the time he came back, I would not still be waiting.

After the first twelve months he came home in the December, just after Christmas, and he said "we're going to get engaged this leave". I didn't want to get engaged, but he insisted. We were engaged on 13th January. My father was livid, "if you marry him he'll bring you to the gutter" he said. Their family and our family were very different, although they were what they were, very ordinary working class people, but Ted shone out. For example he always wore the purest white shirts I ever saw, and I used to wonder however did his mother get them so white. It was a long time after that I discovered he did them himself.

So that was the 13th January and then he was off again for another twelve months. The following January he came home and said

"This leave we are going to get married", I didn't really want to get married at that time. "Well I'm telling you, if we don't get married this leave, I will have my ring back" he said. I looked at the ring, and I looked at him and I thought, I can't give the ring back, so

I'll have to marry him. It was the best days work I ever did.

On the Saturday that we were getting married I was at home getting ready, and for some reason my grandfather was there, as he watched me he said "Where are you going" (neither family knew anything about the wedding), "I'm going to a wedding" I told him. "looks like a posh affair" he said. "Yes, yes it is" I replied.

I would have loved to be able to tell them about the wedding, but I know my mother would have stopped it. So off we went and got married, with just two witnesses. After the ceremony Ted said" what shall we do now", so I said "well I think we should go back and tell my mother". So we went back to the tea gardens and told my mum, who hit the roof. "What you stand up in is what you take from this house" she said, so off we went. We then had to go and tell Ted's mother. "Don't you ever darken our door again, get out and don't darken our door again" she said. We were thrown out of two houses in one day. We decided to go and get something to eat.

I was afraid to order too much because I didn't know how much he had in his wallet.

So we had chips in the Berkley cafe' in Park St. We then wandered back down towards Bedminster, because that's where his roots were. We were feeling rather sad and sorry for ourselves when we met his grandmother, "What's the matter with you two" she asked. "Well we've just got married, and we've been thrown out of both homes. "Oh for Gods sake what's the matter with them, you're coming home with me".

Now Gran was a tough old bird, and she drank whisky like a fish.

Before Ted joined the navy he had never touched alcohol, he drank only water or milk, not even tea or coffee. I recall that when his shipmates found out he didn't drink, as soon as they docked in Grimsby, they whisked him into the nearest pub and plied him with Newcastle Brown ale. He said afterwards that he had never been so ill in his life.

Anyway, back to Grans house. She made us some sandwiches and then out came the whisky bottle. Despite Ted's protests, she insisted we have a drink. "You've just got married, drink up, drink up", so by bed time we were both very much the worse for wear.

So would you believe that I slept in the bed and Ted slept on the floor. "There's no way I'm getting in that bed, no way." So that was our wedding night.

The next morning he's got to go back to Grimsby, so we caught a tram to Temple Meads station. Before he left we both looked in our wallets to see what money we had. We came up with £30 between us. Ted said "I only need £5, you have the rest" and off he went.

I thought I had better try and find some where to live, so I walked up Sandy Park and into Winchester Road, when I got to number 125 I saw a notice saying rooms to let. "Yes my dear, I've got two rooms To let, you share the kitchen and bathroom, you have the front room downstairs and the back bedroom upstairs" said the landlady.

O.K I now have a roof, but I don't have any furniture, so I walked back to Sandy Park, to a little second hand shop. I managed to buy two fireside chairs, a table and four chairs, a cabinet, a bed and a mattress. "Could you please manage to deliver it today" I asked.

"Yes after I shut the shop" and sure enough he did. I also asked if he would take the bed upstairs and assemble it for me.

I had had a long day and decided to go to bed, but I had not got any bedding, just a bare mattress. I rummaged around and found a pile of old newspapers in a cupboard, I wrapped my frock round it to make a pillow, and covered myself with my coat. This is a hard life, I thought.

The next day I got up and went to a caf'e for a cup of tea, and thought I'll go round and see Gramps,(I loved my gran and granddad dearly)

"What, you have got married and not told anyone, how stupid, think of all the presents you could have got." "Gran" I replied, "I don't want anything, I've got Ted and we are going to have a good life".

"Well before you go I'll get granddad to make up a parcel "she said.

So when I got back to Winchester Road, I had two Whitney blankets and a pair of sheets. Oh what luxury.

My granddad was a great inspiration to me as a child. I used to spend a lot of time with him. Always asking questions, "how does this work"? "how does that work"?. One day I asked him if he could explain eternity to me. "Well come into the garden with me" he said, and he pointed to the sky and said "if you look, there's no beginning, and there's no end. Where ever you stand in the world, it's the same. That's the nearest I can get to explaining eternity". He was a great believer in the power of the mind. He told me that whatever I wanted in life, whatever it was, I had to picture it in my mind, and tell myself that it was mine, to own it.

No matter what it was, I could have it. I had to believe and concentrate on it. First thing in the morning and last thing at night. And eventually one day you will own it. This is a tool that I have used many times over the years.

chapter 2

TED'S WAR

In those days when the ships came into port, they were in for a month. But only half the crew could have leave at a time, so the first half would have fourteen days, then the second half would have fourteen days. But if your wife or partner could get to the docks, you could have a month. So when Ted came into Grimsby or wherever I would go up for the month. This particular time, when Ted was going on the first Russian convoy. We were on a train going back from Bristol to Grimsby. There was a chap called Les Kitchen, who was also off the Salamander, and he said "I'm telling you, the Salamander is going down with all hands. I'm not sailing on her, and if you've got any sense Bagsy you won't either". (Bagsy was Teds nick name). So Les decided he was going to jump ship. I asked Ted what he was going to do. Ted said "I'm not jumping ship, if he wants to that's up to him. I'll take my chances".

At this time they did not know that they were going on the first

Russian convoy.

On the way to Mermansk the convoy was being chased by submarines from below and bombers from the air. Forty seven ships were lost in that convoy. The order came to scatter, just go.

So they went into the Norwegian Fjords for a few days. They were then told to regroup, and proceed to Russia. Once more the submarines are stalking them. Another of the ships got torpedoed. The submarine surfaced and picked up the survivors

The sub's captain said that he needed to take the ships captain prisoner. But he gave the crew a life raft, food and water, until they could be picked up. He said that he was sorry for having to sink their ship, and left them.

Ted's ship was told to leave the convoy and go and search for any survivors. After searching for several days, the captain said

"We will have to call off the search or we will not have enough fuel to reach Russia. Just as they were about to get under way somebody spotted a dot on the horizon, and it turned out to be the men on the raft. So they were picked up and taken to Russia on the Salamander.

Les Kitchen, the chap that had jumped ship, had been picked up in Grimsby and sent to Russia to rejoin the Salamander.

The rule was that you had to board your own ship to be weighed off. Kitchen was sentenced to nineteen days, but the Salamander was not large enough to hold anybody in a confined cell. So he was handcuffed and put aboard HMS Bramble, which was going strait back to Devonport. On the way back the Bramble was sunk with all hands. Les Kitchen's premonition was right, but the wrong ship.

At one time they were at Arkangel and the ship was running low on food. The captain decided that if he sent someone ashore they may be able to get some fresh vegetables. As Ted was able to speak a little Russian, it was decided that he would go with one of the officers to see what they could find.

The ice and snow was six feet deep and they could hardly stand.

They proceeded to go in the direction of a small village. As they got close to the village they met an old woman coming towards them. Ted went up to her and tried, by making digging motions, to get across that they wanted vegetables. The old lady beckoned them to follow her. She led them to a large barn type building.

The officer pushed open the doors and ran inside, where he saw a chap laying on a bench, presumably asleep. The officer shook the man to wake up, but he was dead. It turned out to be the local mortuary. She obviously miss interpreted Teds digging action.

They had a good laugh about it afterwards.

They then went into the village, and at a small farm they were able to purchase some potatoes, eggs and vegetables. The crew and the captain were delighted, because for a little while they could have a change from powdered egg and powdered potatoes.

While they were docked there, there were some Finnish prisoners of war, held by the Russians. They used to come down to the dock and scavenge for food in the water between the side of the ship and the dock. This would be food jettisoned from the ship, it was covered in oil and grime. Ted tried to tell them that if they came back the next day he would try and help them. What he did was after the crew had eaten he would scrape the scraps from the plates into a saucepan, heat it up and put into cups which he then gave to the prisoners. They were very grateful and very sad when the Salamander departed.

I had lots of premonitions that Ted was in danger. He used to say that he always saw a bright light over his head, and he used to say to himself, "if I don't see that light, I'm not coming back, as long as I see the light I will be safe". Which he was.

At the time of Dunkirk Ted was on the Salamander, which was a flat bottom boat, and she could go right on to the beach. She was only a small ship with a crew on ninety. They were able to get the chaps that could still walk to climb aboard, and then ferry them to a larger ship anchored off shore. They did this for a number of days.

On the last day at Dunkirk, the Salamander was at the shore next to the Skip Jack, which was a hospital ship. The Skip Jack took a direct hit, a bomb went strait down the funnel, which blew her completely apart. It was a blood bath. The Salamander started to pull away. There were still men coming off the beaches, swimming in the sea. The skipper said, "oh God, we can't leave them, lower a boat Bagsy, lower a boat and pick them up." As Ted went to get in the boat the skipper said "not you Bagsy, not you this time I need you on the rear guns". Ted ran back to the rear gun just as a messershmit dived down and sprayed the boat with it's machine guns. There was Nobby Clark, Maxi Miller and two others in the boat, they were all killed. This was very traumatic for Ted because he would normally have been coxing that boat.

At this time I was telling my granddad that something terrible is happening in a place called Dun something. "There's thousands of men dying, thousands" I told him. "No, no my dear there's nothing like that going on" he said. "Yes there is" I said,

"and Ted is there, I know he is". It was two days later that the news told about the battle of Dunkirk

Later Ted was transferred to an aircraft carrier, HMS Ruler, and sent back and forth to America, ferrying aircraft, we badly needed to gain air supremacy.

On one of these trips, they were in New York on shore leave.

A big burly American approached them and said "hey Limy, would you like something to eat". Having been on ships rations, they said "yes we would love something". So he took them to a restaurant. "Come on in and order whatever you want, don't worry about the cost". So they tucked in, steaks, beer etc. All of a sudden the guy said "take a powder, quick out the back door, take a powder." It turned out the guy didn't have a penny and couldn't pay for any of it. Ted said he had never been so embarrassed in his life.

Eventually HMS Ruler was sent to the far east, and they were in Tokoyo Bay when the Japanese peace treaty was signed. They were told that nobody was to take pictures. Of course Ted took a photograph.

They were then taking on board, the prisoners from the Japanese prisoner of war camps. He said it was heart breaking, the poor creatures were walking skeletons, hardly able to lift their feet.

They were as near to death as they could be. He said that the most tremendous moment, one he will never forget, was bringing the first load of prisoners from Tokoyo in to Sydney harbour. All the ships in the harbour were dressed overall, all the flags and bunting, fire ships with their water cannon firing into the air, and the dock packed with friends, family and well wishers.

On returning from the far east, They docked in Plymouth late at night. There was a telegraph office in the dock, and they all went running down to send word home that they were safe and well.

One of the chaps, Dick Spencer, was running back to the ship when he tripped over a hawser and went head first between the dock and the ship. It was very dark, late at night and he was wearing a heavy overcoat. They just could not get him out. He had just sent a message telling his wife he was coming home, the next telegram was telling her he had drowned.

A similar thing happened to Ted, while they were docked in

London, next to the dry docks. When this is empty there is a drop of about one hundred feet. One day as Ted was training,(he would grab every opportunity to go running or whatever to keep fit). He also tripped over one of the hawsers and went head over heels into the dry dock. As he was falling he thought, this is it,

I'm going to die. At the last minute a rope was put into his hands.

He grabbed the rope and hung on. He was only about six feet from the bottom.

As I said Ted was always very fit. On one of his times in Devonport, the captain was asked if he had any super fit men that could be trained for S.A.S duties, they had to be one hundred percent fit. The captain nominated Ted. They trained twelve hours a day with no let up. The, chap training them was like a wild animal. He was terrible to them, because he had to be, to make them tough enough. Ted was taught to kill a man in three seconds flat. Ted used to say "if that bloke don't end up in the lunatic, asylum, I don't know".

Ted didn't actually join that unit because he was needed back on ship.

chapter 3

MY WAR

While Ted had been away I had moved dozens of times, and

I had also left wills's. I still needed to earn some money as I was now expecting our first baby. I got a job in a factory making cardboard. My aunty was working there and she got me the job. I worked there almost up to the time Michael was born. My aunty loved to knit and she made me the most beautiful shawl.

I moved from Winchester road to 216 Bath road, where I had an upstairs flat, these were very nice, large houses. I am still pregnant with Michael, and very fed up that nothing is happening.

I went round to see my gran, who said "the apple won't fall till it's ready, he'll come when he's ready".

I went to the cinema on Brislington hill and watched a cowboy and indian film. When I got home I'm thinking, O God, how much longer is this going to go on. I found a bottle of caster oil, which I drank. I thought if that doesn't work nothing will.

I packed my bag and got everything ready then went to bed.

About 5am, I'm feeling a bit uncomfortable and thought I'd better go round to the nursing home, which was in the next road,

9 Hampstead road. (that 9 crops up a lot). So I got up and dressed and off I go. I managed to get round to the nursing home. The lady that opened the door took one look at me and whisked me strait up to the delivery room. Michael was born at mid day.

While I was in the nursing home we had a couple of air raids. We had to get out of bed, and under the protective covers, which were like big metal tables. The idea was that if the ceiling fell down, you weren't hit by falling rubble or plaster.

My grandmother was determined that she was going to carry the baby home, no one else, she was going to be the one.

Because she was so proud and fussy with everything, all the curtains had to be taken down and washed, before baby came home. Unfortunately she fell off the steps when she was taking down the curtains. That was the end of her carrying baby, so my mother came to do it.

I wasn't at Bath Rd very long, because my mother wanted me to move nearer to Beese's tea gardens. On the day I was moving,

Ted came home on leave, just as the chaps were taking out the furniture. "We can't get the wardrobe out" said the men, "it won't come over the stairs". Ted said "I'll show you what to do", he opened the french doors, onto the balcony. He got some electrical cable that was there, tied it to the wardrobe and proceeded to lower it over the balcony. As it's dangling in mid air, a bus was coming by and the driver stopped the bus to watch. "What's the matter with them" Ted said, "haven't they seen anyone move a wardrobe before". We were moving to Birchwood Rd.

From Bircchwood Rd, I moved to Bingham, where Ted's aunty had recently bought a house, so I moved in there, but it only lasted about a month, we just couldn't get on at all.

I then moved to 147 Ashton Drive, again two rooms. The lady had a little boy the same age as Michael. I remember one day having almost no money, and my allowance wasn't due until the next day. I had just enough to buy either potatoes or bread. I stood outside the shop thinking bread or potatoes, potatoes or bread. I ended up buying the bread. I still think of that whenever I pass that shop. We stayed at Ashton Drive quite a while. Just before Ted was due for demob, I moved to 46 Hamilton Rd, where I was fortunate enough to rent the whole house. So when Ted came out of the navy we were able to have a whole house to our selves for the first time ever. While Ted had been in Australia, our second child, Diane, was born in 1943.

chapter 4

CIVVY STREET

Before Ted had left Australia, he had the presence of mind to stock up on food that he knew we could not get here. Tins of ham, corned beef, tinned fruit etc.

They docked at Plymouth. My family had a friend called

Albert Mason who had been in Australia at the same time as

Ted. And he lived in Plymouth, so he said to Ted "why not ask

Edith to come down and stay with the wife and I for a few days".

It was going to take a few days for Ted to get his final demob sorted.

So I went down to Plymouth and we stayed with the Masons.

This was a big mistake, because Ted now had all the food he'd brought from Australia, at Albert's house. "O Ted, you've got corned beef, O Ted you've got this and you've got that". Albert had exactly the same chance to do what Ted had done but he hadn't bothered. So silly Ted is giving them all our food.

Before we left Plymouth to return home, Ted had stupidly said to Albert that they must come and spend a few days in Bristol. Not thinking they would take up the offer. It was just after Christmas and we had been home about a couple of days when we got a call from Albert saying they were coming up to Bristol, "is that O.K". Well it wasn't but we had invited them so O.K. We expected them to stay for a couple of days, but no, they stayed well over a week. Eat all our remaining food, or at least, tried to. Piled the fire with precious coal, that I had saved up. Finally on the day of their departure they set off for Temple Meads station to get the train. Ted said "O thank God for that, let's have a cup of tea, and I'll put some music on the gramophone". "Come on" he said "lets have a dance". So we are dancing away, and the door bell goes. Albert and his wife had missed the train, so we had them for another night. The next day we made sure they caught their train.

So that was us settling back in to married life with our son

Michael, who was born in 1940.

When Ted came home from the war, he was very difficult to live with for the first few months. His nerves were shot to pieces. Every time he heard a bell or a loud noise it would really make him jump.

After his demob, Ted went back to work at Marsdon's, so I said "I'm going to look for a job, I don't know what, but I will get something". I ended up getting a job in a laundry, in North Street, Ashton. It was only a couple of streets away so I could easily walk to work. I got on quite well and became a supervisor. Which isn't as grand as it sounds, because you' are really just a dogs body. If someone does not turn up to open one of the other shops, then you have to go and do it.

Ted kept saying that he wondered what had happened to all those souls that had just passed. Was there really anything beyond?. He could never lose his faith in a God, and he could not accept that there was nothing beyond life.

One evening we sat talking until about 10pm, I said O.K I don't want to talk any more about the spirit world, I'm going to bed". About ten minutes later Ted came up and got in to bed.

A few minutes later, hovering in the air above the bed, was what looked like a hollow bamboo cane. It started tapping.

"Now look what you've done" I said, Ted said "no, be quiet, it's tapping out morse code". (he had learnt mors in the navy).

What he got was part of a surname and part of a first name, it didn't make any sense at the time. Then just as quickly it faded away. I am convinced that there is some sort of jiggery pokery going on. I tried to move the wardrobe, then the dressing table, looking for some sort of explanation where the cane had come from. Ted said "just get back in bed and accept that it is spirit".

A couple of days later Ted bumped into his sister, Iris. He told her the story of the cane. She said "Ted you really need to go and talk to Mrs Bugden, she's a medium and runs the sweet shop on the corner of Phillip St. Go and have a chat to her." He was very apprehensive. Any way he went in and Mrs. Bugden said "you're Iris's brother, I've been waiting for you". "Have you", he said. "Yes" she said, "there's an Indian stood by you."

Ted looked around and thought what is she on about, an Indian.

"You must come and sit in our circle, and let's find out more".

"Oh I don't know about that", Ted said. "Yes, you must come on Wednesday afternoon, after I shut the shop. We hold the circle in my dining room."

Ted came home and told me that he would have to get time off on Wednesday. "How do you think we can afford for you to have half a day off" I said. "Well, she said I've got to be there, so I think I will have to go.

So Wednesday comes around and off he goes. There were seven or so people there, sat around a big solid oak table. It must have been about 4 inches thick.

She said" We'll open in prayer, and then see what happens. Just place your fingertips lightly on the table. As they sat there she started saying "Come on friend, come along now". Ted is thinking, if she thinks this table is going to move, she is barmy. All of a sudden the table start rapping, "your spelling out a name" she said. She told Ted what letters were being spelled-out. To his surprise, it was the same letters he had got from the cane and our bedroom. It turned out that his name was Hagar Geiger, and he was an Egyptian. He turned out to be a wonderful friend to us over the years.

After we had the visitation in the bedroom with the cane, Ted very much wanted to go to a Spiritualist Church. We discovered there was one in Prewett Street, near where we lived. On the Sunday night Ted asked me to go with him, but I did not want to go. "You go, and tell me about it when you come home" Apparently he got a message, and came home absolutely bubbling. "You've got to come next week, even if you only come the once, you've got to come and see what it's about".

The following Sunday I plucked up courage and went. I sat at the back, hoping the medium would not find me. But of course, I got the most tremendous message, the first message I had ever had. I couldn't understand some of the things she said. She was saying that I had an auntie Martha, to which I said no. In fact I said no to most of the things she said. She gave me a reading which amounted to what I would be doing the rest of my life. When we came out, my sister, who was not brave enough to come to the service was waiting for us. "How did you get on" she asked. "Well, I don't know" I said. "She talked about an auntie Martha, we haven't got an aunt Martha have we"? She said "Don't be stupid, of course we have. She is head postmistress at Chew Magna". The medium had said whoever Martha was, had had a government stamp. Of course the Post Office had a government stamp.

After that we started going to Spiritualist churches in the area. We wanted to know more. We went to the church in Prewett Street, Bedminster, one

Sunday morning. As we sat in the church, a chap came in and sat behind us. "You should not be here" he said. "Shouldn't we" we replied. "No, no, you should be in Surrey house, St Paul's". We said "why is that"? "Because there's a man there called Ernie Oaton, who used to be the editor of Two Worlds, and he is waiting to talk to you". We hadn't a clue who Ernie Oaton was, but the next time there was a service Surrey house we were there. That was their first introduction to Ernie

It was while we were attending Surrey house, we were told that we were both healers. One of the people that was training us was very vindictive, "Those two must never be allowed to work together, they are both very powerful healers and must never work together".

While working in the laundry shop one day, Florie Burrows came in holding her stomach. "Oh what's the matter my dear" I asked.

She said "I'm in terrible pain, I have to go in for an operation in a weeks time for gall stones". I said "Come round the counter, let me see if I can help". She came behind the counter and I gave her healing. I asked where she lived and she told me it was over Lloyds bank. "Well when I shut the shop I'll come round" I said.

I went round every night until the Thursday. She said "I'm out of pain, I've thrown all my tablets away, and I feel marvellous"

"That's great "I replied. On the Friday morning, her husband Cliff came in to see me and said "Florie's so much better, do you think it would be alright to take her away for the weekend". "That would be marvellous" I said, "Where are you going"? "My aunty has a cottage in the country, there is no running water, no proper toilet, but it's just beautiful". So off they went. On the Saturday night as they lay in bed, about three O'clock in the morning, Florie woke him and said "Cliff, Cliff I've messed the bed". "Don't be silly" he said. "Yes, put your hand down, it's all like glue, and it feels like hands in my stomach. Can't you smell it". "Yes" he said, "it smells vile"

He got out of bed and lit the oil lamp, pulled back the covers, and there was nothing there. The bed was clean. They settled down and went to sleep. They returned home on the Sunday, and Monday morning she came in to tell me the story. "That's wonderful" I said,

"What you had was a spirit operation". She had to go to the hospital on Tuesday for her pre op. The doctor said "we just want to do some tests before tomorrows op" They did the tests and took an X-ray.

The doctor said "I wont be operating". "Why is that" she asked, "What's wrong". He showed her the X-ray and said "The gall stones have gone".

That was my undoing, I don't know what happened, I can't claim any credit for it. All I know is that I introduced her to the spirit healers and they obviously took it into their own hands to remove them. The jealousy that came from that beggars belief. People that had taught me, and I thought were close, were the ones that turned the knife. I just could not believe it.

Apart from our Thursday night healing sessions at home, people were coming in saying they knew of other people that would like to have healing, but they just can't get to you. We decided that we would get on our bicycles and go round giving healing in peoples homes. At this time I was still at the laundry. Ted would meet me after I closed the shop, and we would bike round the houses. Some times there may be twelve and some times as many as eighteen calls to make. Quite often we would get to the house and the people would say, "Were watching something on T.V, or wev'e got visitors, can you leave it this week".

After doing this for about eighteen months, I said to Ted one night,

"We've got it wrong, these people are just sitting at home waiting for us to come and perform miracles and they are putting no effort in to it. This week we will tell them that in future, healing will take place in our house on a Thursday evening between five thirty and eight o'clock. With the exception of those that are house bound or bedridden".

For the first couple of weeks only a few turned up but we had some very good results, and word soon spread and it grew.

I arrived at Surrey house one afternoon, and there was no medium. Mrs Howells said "I'm so glad you've come Edith, the medium has not turned up, and there's no one to take the service. You've been sitting in circle for three years, surely you could take the service". I said "Well, if you've got the guts to ask me, I've got the guts to do it". For some reason Ted was not with me that day. I took the service. When we finished we went downstairs to the committee room.

We had a very sour faced spinster lady that was a church treasurer, Miss Gray. Mrs Howells said "oh, Miss Gray, wasn't that wonderful. Mrs Baker was able to take that service right through. I'm so pleased, it was marvellous. Miss Gray never looked up, she said "mushroom growth, neither good to garden or man". That really put me down.

The very first funeral I took was a lady called Mrs Duncan. We had been sat in circle at Surrey house on the Tuesday evening, it was a dreadful November night. It was cold, it was raining, it was miserable. The next morning the phone rang and it was Mrs Duncan son, "I'm very sorry to tell you Mrs B, my mum had an accident on the way home last night. She fell off the back of the bus in Cranbrook Road, and broke her neck, she died instantly. I am ringing to ask if you would take her funeral service". I said "I've never taken a funeral service before". He said "she would love it if you did, please say you will do it". So I did. It was the very first funeral service at Surrey house.

I also took the first one at Cairns Road. Jeff Bosley, Jeff and Grace Bosley were both strong members of Cairns Road Church. They had gone on holiday to Bournemouth, on the Saturday afternoon. All excited because they were going for a fortnight. Jeff was pushing Grace along the seafront in her wheelchair, when he collapsed and died. I took the funeral service.

It was about this time that I had a falling out with the management of the laundry company. At the end of each week I had to balance the books. If you were short you had to put the money in. But if you were over, you had to pay that money into the bank. This particular week I just could not get the books to balance. I had £17.50 more money than I should have had. I told Ted about it, and he suggested I should put the money in an envelope under the counter. "Next week when you do the balance, you will probably find it". "No Ted, I can't do that, I've got to pay it in". I decided to phone the boss, Mr Heiden, and tell him. "Well" he said, "you know what you have to do, you must pay it in", so I did.

Not the next week, but two weeks later, I balance the books and I was £17.50 p short. So again I phoned Mr Heiden and told him." Well" he said "you know what you have to do, you must make up the shortfall". I said "thank you very much Mr Heiden, if you would like to come and collect the keys, I won't be opening the shop on Monday". "You can't do that" he said. I replied "I'm sorry, but you don't trust me, and I'm not comfortable working for you.

So I am now out of work

Ted had a again joined the boxing club at Marsden's, and he got on very well. He was always out at different boxing bouts. He was very successful. One night he was fighting at the Morris car factory in Swindon. My father still had no time for Ted, but being an ex-boxer he used to go to the fights.

On this particular occasion, Ted's second said "Charlies on the train, what if I ask him to be your second tonight".

My father agreed to do it,. And before the fight started he came and sat by me." Do you know the name of the other fighter" he asked. I said" yes its Jenkins, something ".Are you sure," he said, "if that's the son of who I think it is, Ted's got no chance".

When the bout started, it was a case of bang bang, bang bang, and who went through the ropes? Jenkins, out cold, and who ended up fighting? My father and Jenkins father.

I always used to go to the fights, which proved to be quite useful. On one occasion they were fighting down at Avonmouth, in the metal works. As I set waiting for the fight to start, Onslow Carey, the director of Marsden's came and sat by Me.

A few days prior to this, Ted had put in a holiday request, via Mr Fletcher his foreman. Fletcher hated Ted, because he didn't like the fact the directors would come down and talk to Ted about boxing.

Onslow said how's things Blondie, I said "okay, just a couple of problems". "Such as", he said, "well" I said, "we've requested a couple of weeks holiday in August, but Mr Fletcher said we can't have it" "Oh", he said," what were the dates". So I told him.

On the following Monday morning, Onslow was down in the office talking to Fletcher. The next thing Ted knows, Fletcher came over to him, and said "I've been looking at those dates you wanted, and it will be all right for You to have them". This did not go down very well with Fletcher, and he did everything he could to make Ted's life unbearable.

One Friday night Ted came home as white as a sheet. "What ever is the matter" I asked. He said "I'm going to kill him". "No you are not" I said. "Tomorrow morning you are going to hand in your notice". "I can't do that" he said, "what will we do"? I said, "never mind what we will do, you'r giving in your notice". Which he did.

Different families

Ted and I came from two very different backgrounds. I was going out with him before my seventeenth birthday and he decided

I had to have some roses. His mother was sent to buy a dozen and a half roses, but couldn't understand why she had to get rid of one, hence seventeen roes, (every year since I would be given the appropriate number of roses, ie 21 or 25 whatever).

I could never understand why he never invited me to his home to meet his family. He had met all my family.

One Saturday he met me off the bus, we then caught a tram to go into the centre of Bristol. I noticed that he seemed very uncomfortable and he was blushing. There was a lady at the far end of the tram, hair in curlers and wearing a long rain coat. When the tram stopped and we got off, the lady was standing waiting. "Ted, Ted" she said, "Now you've got to introduce me to her". So Ted said "this is my mother"

"Oh pleased to meet you" I said. She asked "Why is our Ted not bringing you home to meet us?" (I wanted to say, because he's never asked me, but I didn't). So she said "You've got to come home, we want to meet you", "yes", I said, "that would be nice". "Right" she replied, "next Saturday, he's got to bring you home for a cup of tea".

The following Saturday he met me off the bus and we walked round to Phillip Street, where he lived. Once inside the house, I realised why he had not asked me before. They lived in such poor conditions.

They had one room that was O.K for visitors, but the rest of the house was not to be talked about. It was just a typical two up, two down with an outside toilet.

At the end of the day, he said," if you don't want to see me again, I will fully understand". But I thought more of him than ever.

A short while after that it was coming up to Trafalgar day and he said

"I'm playing in Bath Abbey, I'm a bugler in the R.N.V.R band, and we're marching through Bath, then attending the Trafalgar day service In the Abbey. I'm playing the last post and reveille on the bugle".

The accoustics of the bugle in the Abbey was just breath taking. From then on I was completely hooked.

When my mother was born she was the first of my grandmothers children. Gran was very proud and she had one of those big silver cross prams with a huge wheels. When my mother was about six weeks old, a young girl they know came round and asked if she could take the baby for a walk. Yes you could take her out" said grandmother.

The girl pushed the pram down to the main road where there were deep Tram tracks. Unfortunately the pram wheels caught in the tracks, tipping the pram over. The pram fell across my mother's back, (these prams were very heavy). Instead of telling anyone, the girl decided to keep quiet about it.

Every time my grandmother touched the baby, she would scream with pain. It was only after about a week later they took baby to hospital, to discover that her hip bone was crushed. She was a cripple for the rest of her life and walked with a limp.

Because her parents thought she could never work in a factory, or do anything physical, they looked for something a little more genteel. They managed to get her an apprenticeship with a famous Bristol milliners. She was very, very clever with a needle, and made the most fantastic hats, the sort of thing you see at Ascot, on ladies day. She was also very fond of music, again because her father thought she would never make much of her life, he sent her to music lessons. Her teacher said that she was brilliant, and ought to have her own piano at home, to work with. Which they got. On a Sunday night, they would push the piano to the front of the shop, and all the neighbours would come down for a singsong.

She continued to study music, and actually got a degree.

After she met my father, (I'm not sure how they met) they eventually decided to get married, which they did, without telling anyone. They then came back and told the family. Beeses tea gardens had the main house, and a separate cottage in the grounds. This was where they were going to live. She thought that because the piano was bought for her, and none of the other girls were interested in music, she would take it with her. Her father had different ideas, no, no way are you taking the piano. There are the other girls coming up, the piano stays here.

She was so bitter about this that she never, ever played another note.

So when I say that she was a hard, bitter lady, that is why she was the way she was. She would have been a very good dancer. She was tall, and always most elegantly dressed. Every thing had to be colour coordinated. I've know her say to me "I've walked Bristol,

I've walked Bath and I've walked Clevedon, I just can't get a bag to match these shoes.

26

The papers

We had been in Hamilton Road about twelve months or so, always looking for an extra shilling. When I discovered that the government were looking for digs, (accommodation), for chaps coming out of the forces. Many of these men had joined up at sixteen or seventeen, during the war, and had no qualifications of any kind. So the government set up a residential training centre in Bristol, where they could train as plumbers, carpenters, or whatever. They would be at the centre for six months or a year to gain a qualification.

Not satisfied with four, I decided we would have six of these chaps, coming and living in our house. Which meant I had to go and buy six beds, rearrange the furniture, and Ted and I moved to a room downstairs. We had a lady that used to come in each day to make the beds and help with breakfast.

The men would have their mid day meal at the centre, then come home for a cooked dinner in the evening. Mrs. Prossor, who lived in the next road would come round to help prepare and serve the meal, and wash the dishes.

So I did have help, but it was hard work. This went on for quite a while.

Eventually I said to Ted, "I don't think we'll have any more, once this batch leave, we'll find something different", Ted was still at Marden's at this time. I had been looking in the newspaper to try and find another way to make a shilling. There was a newspaper round for sale, 1,000 customers, and he wanted £260 for the round. His name was Mr. Hale.

I got in touch with him, and he came to see me. He assured me that it was dead easy, I could do it standing on my head.

He had ten boys, and a spare, for the deliveries, and he would take me out and show me the rounds. He also said that he would come with me for the first month to show me the ropes, (he hardly came with me the first week). I had to be up at five am, catch the bus across Bristol to

Southmead, and meet the boys on the corner of Kaybart Road. We would do the morning rounds and then go back again for the evening papers. So twice a day I'm busing across Bristol.

The first morning that I was on my own it was pissistantly raining

(this is not a spelling mistake), it was chucking it down. Oh well welcome to the real world.

Only nine of the boys turned up, and no spare. I would have to do the round for the missing boy.

I have to walk, Stanstead Rd, Felstead Rd, Kayne Park, Ambleside, etc.

At midday I ended up pushing the last soaking wet paper through the letter box. A womans voice screeched out "we're used to early morning papers," So I shouted back," Well this is early afternoon papers". I staggered down the road to a telephone box, rang for a taxi and went home. Ted saw the taxi draw up, (he was at home for his lunch)

"What ever is the matter" he asked. I relayed the story of the mornings events. "And I've got to go back again tonight" I said. "You're not going back, you're not doing that again", he said. "I'm going round to see Dr. Cussons, I'm going on the sick", he said, so off he went.

"Oh doctor, I've got a really bad back, I can hardly stand" he told her.

"Mr. Baker, you can't possibly work like that, I'll give you a sick note for four weeks, that's going to take a long time to sort out".

So for the next month he was back and forth across Bristol with me.

We decided that the best thing to do was to buy a little 'Corgi',

(These were little motor scooters originally made for paratroopers)

Now I thought that fully comprehensive meant that anyone could ride it, but no, it was in my name only. One night as I'm coming down

Gloucester Road, a car shot out in front of me and knocked me for six. I couldn't walk, or hardly stand. They wanted to take me to hospital, but I said no "just take me home". So the car driver took me and the 'Corgi' home.

The next morning I could hardly move, I certainly couldn't do the papers. So Ted set off on the 'Corgi' to go and do them. He was stopped by a policeman who asked to see the insurance, that's when we found he was not covered. He was given a month in prison.

I don't know how I got through that month. The people from Surrey house offered to help, but none of them did, any way, I got through it.

Ouija board

One day, after Ted had left Mardens, my sister came and asked

"What are you going to do now?" I said "I don't know, I've got the papers. That's going well but it 's not enough to support both of us". So she said "well my chimney sweep is selling up, he wants to emigrate". "Oh does he" I said, "do you know how much he wants for it". "It's a thriving business" she said "I think he wants £300 or so". "Well ask him to come round and see us" I said. So he came round and we talked about it. I asked Ted

"What do you think". I'll have a go at anything" he replied.

The following Thursday, as we sat in circle, I said to our guide,

"I've got the papers, and Teds going to have the sweeps business, what do you think?." The guide replied "It's going to be really hard work, but it will be very profitable, and many people will be helped because of this". I thought, what does he mean, many people will be helped? (But of course looking back now, I can see that many people have been helped).

We purchased the sweep business, which was the first vacuum sweep in Bristol. Ted was going to start on the coming Monday.

On the Saturday before, he was fairly confident but felt he would like a practice run. I pointed to the grate and said, "Practice away".

So he got the vacuum machine in, got the brushes, and sealed off the fire place, all set.

He sent Michael to the bottom of the garden, Diane was positioned half way up the garden, and I stood by the door. The idea was that when the brushes appeared out the chimney Michael would shout to Di and she would shout to me. So away he went, pushing the rods up. Suddenly Micheal is shouting, stop, stop!. "Whatever is the matter"

Ted asked. Michael said, "The brush has just come out of the chimney two houses down the road. We all ran to look, and there it was. It turned out that another sweep was working down the road.

Along with the business came a little Commer van. we were saving to buy a car, but in the meantime what Ted would do was hose the van down inside and out. Put two boxes in the back, with a plank across covered with blankets. That was the seat for me and the children when we went out anywhere.

One sunday we got a phone call from Eddie Howell, the organist at Surrey Road church. He said that he could not pick the medium up because his car had broken down. Could we collect her and take her to the church. We arrived at the address, in the sweeps van.

She was not amused. She was a frightfully, awfully, type, wearing a pair of pristine white gloves. We explained, as she looked down her nose. Eddie's car had broken and it was the sweeps van or nothing.

She very reluctantly got in. Now no matter how much you clean a sweeps van you ca'nt get every little bit of soot out. Needless to say that when we reached the church, the white gloves were any thing but pristine.

About this time my sister got married, my mother and father were very much against the man she was marrying because he was Polish. Like Ted and I, they just went out and married. They moved in with us and rented two rooms. My sister was very dry, very strict like my mother. She couldn't see the sun if it shone in her face Next door was a family of three daughters, mum and dad. Every Sunday they went to church, and returned home about a quarter to nine. Then the ding dong would start. "Oh, mother he can't have fried bread, you know what it does to his indigestion". "Oh, for Gods sake Alice, let him have some fried bread". This went on for quite a time. Two wanted him to have fried bread and two did not. After a while my sister threw open the bedroom window, which overlooked next doors garden, and shouted, "For Gods sake, give him some fried bread and let us all get some peace".

On the other side was a family where the father was always drunk.

He would come home rolling drunk and throw them out into the street. The lady that lived the other side of them had had enogh.

She wasn't going to put up with it. She went in and said to Gwyneth, the wife. "If he comes in tonight and starts, I will give him what for. About eleven O'clock the husband came home drunk, shouting and carrying on. The next thing, not only his wife but the neighbour as well, were thrown into the street.

At one of our Tuesday evening circles, my sister Dorothy and husband Larion sat watching. When the guide said, "Larion, sit at the table". This was the first time we had ever had the ouija board. A relative came through for him, and said they had been on a barge on the Rhine, transporting coal from Poland. They were attacked by the Luftwaffe, who sank the boat, and they were both drowned. Larion said" I don't recall any relative doing that". But the spirit was determined this was the case, and then went on to add that in a weeks time, he would receive a letter from Poland telling him about this. Larion replied" I've not had a letter from Poland since I've been here, and I don't expect to get one now". A week later he got a letter from Poland.

When Larion" big farm in Poland, one Sunday morning as they sat having lunch, the German soldiers arrived. The two boys one was 16 and the other 17, were taken at bayonet point to a nearby pond, where they were held overnight. The next morning they were both taken before the commandant, and Heinrich said it was the biggest shock of his life, to find that this had been his schoolteacher.

Larion met and married Dorothy, and his brother, Heinrich went to Notts where he met a young lady and they got engaged. The day before they were due to get married, she dropped down dead from a heart attack. He was devastated, and decided to return to Poland. When he wrote to Larion, he told him, "don't ever think of coming back here, your life in England is so much better, don't even think of it.

Also at that same circle, my brother John was home on leave. He was part of an army motorcycle display team, they used to do all sorts of stunts, riding standing on their heads, all sorts. That night he had returned to Aldershot, and we were told through the ouija board, there had been an accident and John had been killed. We were beside ourselves, and didn't know what to do. I decided to phone the police to see if they could check it out. Eventually they rang back and said he was fine, he had arrived back safely. And that was the first and last time we have used the ouija board.

At this time, I'm thinking, we can't go on commuting back and forth to Southmead, some thing has to be done, we had to move.

There were some very nice houses on Southmead Road, and I was very drawn to 351. Using the power of the mind, I decided that's the one I'm going to have. I started concentrating on it, and I concentrated, and concentrated. I said to Ted, "we've got to move to Southmead Road some how, I don't know how, but wev'e got to do it". "Well I don't know how" he said, "you would need a deposit". "I don't care" I said, "it will come from some where". So I found an estate agent and asked if they ever had any houses come up on Southmead Rd. They had houses in southmead, but it was very seldom they got any on Southmead road. They said they would let me know if one came up. The very next morning he was knocking at our door. "I've got a house on Southmead Road" he said. I said "don't tell me, it's 351" "How do you know that" he asked.? "It is" I said, "It's 351

34

isn't it"? He said "Yes it is, I'll take you out and show you it". I stood on the doorstep and I said "I'm buying it". "But you have not seen it yet" he said. "Yes I have" I replied, "I can describe every room, I'm buying it" and the deal was done. We had had a lot of good times at Hamilton road, we had lots of family parties. Teds sister was the only one with any music, she had a gramophone that she would put on an old pram and push round to our house. Ted was the life and soul of the party, he would get every one going. All the children would be in one room with lemonade and stuff, and the adults in another, letting their hair down, and did they let their hair down.

Now I've got to find the deposit, which I don't have, and I'm thinking, what am I going to do?. I phoned my mother, and told her what I was trying to do. And said I needed some money. "We'll lend you £100, that's all we can do, and you'll have to pay it back". It was Friday, and Mr. Howden, the landlord, called for the rent. I told him we were trying to move. "Well what's stopping you" he asked? "Well there's the small matter of finding the deposit" I said. "Well if your out in six weeks I'll give you £150, but it must be within six weeks" he said. I thought £150 plus £100 from my mother, were on our way. It still wasn't enough. I wondered, if I rang the newspapers to see if they would grant me some time to pay. I phoned The News of The World, the Daily Express and the Guardian, and I explained the situation and asked if it was possible for me to have a months credit.

In those days if you did not have bricks and mortar, you could not get credit. Because I was such a good customer and the business was growing, they all gave me credit for a month. So I had the money from the papers, the money from Mr. Howden, and the promise of money from mother. We were getting there, it's coming together. Then mother decides, she can't do it, "we've been thinking about it all night, and we just can't do it. There's your brother and your sisters, and we just can't do it". "That's O.K, don't worry" I said. I went ahead and got everything organised, the removal van etc. On the Friday I went to the solicitors office with the deposit, to complete the deal. I was thrilled to bits. I told the solicitor, "I've come to pay the deposit, I know the mortgage is arranged and everything, but I've made a terrible mistake". "Oh, what's that" he asked. I said "I forgot that you have to be paid" "Yes my dear, I'm sorry but we do have to get paid" "Well I'm sorry I can't do it, I just don't have any more money" I told him.

"Oh, dear me" he said "Oh dear". He put his hand down and opened a drawer and took out the keys, which he handed to me.

"You've got an honest face my dear, pay me when you've got it".

"How much is it" I asked? He replied "It's £80, but don't worry, pay me when you can".

On the Saturday morning we were all set. The van was loaded with our bits and pieces, including two bantams in a cage. We arrived at 351 and moved our stuff in, including some orange boxes, to use as side tables etc. We settled down, and football was on. When the days results were given, Ted said "I don't know how to tell you, but wev'e won the pools". "Don't be daft" I told him. "Yes we have, wev'e won" he said. It was a bad day as far as football was concerned, lots of matches had been cancelled due to the weather. "I don't know how much it will be, we'll have to wait until Wednesday" he said.

In my mind, from the Saturday to the Wednesday, I had bought up half of Bristol, new car, the lot. Wednesday morning the cheque arrived, I could hardly wait as Ted opened it. "Well" he said,

"It's eighty six pounds three shillings and ten pence, I know where the eighty pounds is going, I know where the six pounds is going, but that three shillings and ten pence, is worrying me to death.

One of the first things I discovered when we moved in, was that the next door but one neighbour, had a news agents in the adjoining shops. He was not best pleased because he could see the delivery boys coming and going. There were two people in opposition to us.

One was Mr. Phillips that had the shop and had very big rounds, and there was another chap that just had a few smaller rounds.

Our business was growing and growing. There was an estate at the top of the road, called Henbury. The boys would watch for new people moving in, and then ask them for their paper order. The draw was that the boys would get the first weeks paper money as a bonus, this could be two or three shillings, which in those days was quite a lot. They were dead keen to get the business.

We were at Southmead Road quite a while. We held circle on Tuesday evening and healing on Thursdays, at weekends we were travelling to various churches. Although we were earning, we still didn't have a lot of money to spare

I said to our guide, "We need to have a business which will give us sufficient money, that we never have to ask for travelling expenses, or a fee for our services". The guide said "That's a tall order but we will endeavour to give you the answer next week".

The following Tuesday we were sat in a circle, and the guide came through and said "you have to start a ladder hire business". I thought, what the devil is that." It will give you sufficient money to do what you wish". He said. So we talked about it. And I asked Ted what he thought," well you either believe them or you don't, if you do, go with it, if you don't, just walk away".

I looked in the telephone book under ladders, and found the Eclipse ladder company in Bristol. I phoned them up and spoke to the director. I said "I'm thinking of starting a ladder hire business." "I've never heard of that before," he said. "No neither have I" I replied. He arranged to send his rep over to see me, and I explained what the idea was. A lot of chaps were returning from the war, and wanting to paint their houses, but they didn't have a ladder. And couldn't afford to buy one.

He asked how much money I had to spend. And I told him it was £75." Okay" he said, "we will stretch it as far as we can".

The ladders were duly delivered. Between sorting out the papers, and doing the books, etc. I was out in the yard painting the ladders. I painted one side black and the other side blue. Ted came home and asked "why are you painting them black and blue". Because that's the colour I'll be after I've delivered them" I replied.

I went round all the local shops putting cards in the Windows at three pence a week, advertising ladder hire. Our insurance agent, Mr Gadd came round one day and asked what all the ladders were doing in the yard. So I explained." No one will ever hire ladders" he said. Guess who are first customer was? Mr Gadd.

I told Ted that I wasn't happy the way things were going. I had five pounds left, and I told him I was going down to the Bristol Evening Post and buying the biggest advert I could. Which I did. After that we never looked back. The business took off and we bought a little Commer 5 hundredweight van. I had not passed my test, but I'm driving it anyway. I would pick Diane up from school, set her on a pile of cushions, and tell her to look intelligent. That was the start of ladder higher

Shortly after we acquired ladder hire, which was financing our spiritual work. We received a letter from Mr Croker, at Surrey house, asking me to attend a medium's meeting. The letter was unsigned. Ted said" that's very rude, not to sign it. I would not go if I were you". "Yes I'm going, I want to know what it's all about" I replied. When I got there there were several mediums from the south-west present, and its chairman, Simon Croker.

When I walked in the talking stopped. There was a deathly hush. I said to Mr Croker "excuse me, but I think this meeting is about me and my husband". He started coughing and spluttering. I said" For God sake, whatever it is, say it". He then said "It has been brought to the attention of the committee, that you and your husband have been taking services, without asking for a fee or travelling expenses. Is that correct". "Yes, that is correct, is there a law against it" I replied. More coughing and spluttering, "well no, but I suggest you change your mind and start conforming like everybody else. It's just not fair. Mediums will not be asked to take services, if you and Mr Baker are doing it for free. I said" I'm very sorry Mr Croker, but I will not be changing my mind". So then they started, we have to go and get her hair done." Well don't you think I have to get my hair done" I replied. We have to get our clothes cleaned, and so it went on and on. Such bitchiness. I was realy disappointed, as I thought I'd found this wonderful proof, this between people, and it wasn't at all. I said "Thank you very much Mr Croker. I am leaving" and I went. As I was walking back to get the bus, crying, a lady came up behind me. "Change your mind my dear, change your mind, they will crucify you" I said" They did that to someone else once.

When I got home I was in a real state. Ted said "What's the matter" I said "I am never going to take another spiritualist church as long as I live, never". "Hang on a minute, that's what they want you to do. If you don't take another spiritualist church I will. I'm not going to be dictated to" Three months later we were taking the service in Cairns Road. It was Sunday morning, Ted gave the address as usual and everything is going fine. I gave a message to a lady. I said "it's very unusual for me, but I don't see this gentleman that is coming through". So I described him to her, and said, "what he's saying is, please don't change the way you work, please keep going as you are, that is what the spirit people want and they will support you every step of the way. So I finished the clairvoyance and closed the service. As I came down off the rosteram the lady I had given the message to approach me and said "Mrs Baker, you don't know who I am do you" I said "No, I don't know who you are". She said "I'm Simon Croker's wife, he died three weeks ago, and that message was for you my dear, not me.

Mr Phillips, the newsagent, went bankrupt. Somehow my mother got wind of this, before it became generally known. His shop was number 451, just along the road from our house. "You've got to get that shop, whatever it costs, you've got to get it"." But we have not got that sort of money, even for the deposit" I said. "We will lend you £150", she said.

So I made the usual noises to the selling agent, and arranged to see the bank manager for a loan. He was a very dour face Scott. My appointment was for 9:30 Monday morning. As I was getting ready on the Monday, the phone rang,. And it was my mother "Sorry, we can't lend you the £150". I thought, she's done it again.

I sat wondering what to do, when Chan, my Chinese guide said "Ring Bill Pope", Bill was a cousin of Teds, he was a motor engineer and had a Garage and workshops in Bristol. I thought, what have I got to lose. So I plucked up courage and phoned him." Hello Blondie, why are you phoning me this hour of the day". So I explained to him what had happened with mother, and that I needed some money for the shop deposit." What time is your appointment at the bank" he asked. I told him." Okay, I'll meet you outside the bank".

Bill was a real grease monkey. He drove the most beautiful sports car, absolutely pristine, but he looked every bit a grease monkey. When we went in to see the bank manager he looked down his nose at us, as if we had crawled out from under a stone. He did not want to know. Bill said "How much does she need". The manager did his sums and told us how much I would need. "That's all right" said Bill." I will stand guarantor for any amount you want, whatever you ask for". The manager completely changed his attitude, signed the papers, and I bought the shop.

I repaid the loan within three months

It was around this time, 1955, that we had our first cruise. It came about because Bill Pope and his wife were going to be celebrating their silver wedding, and were planning to go on a cruise. Ted said" I wouldn't mind doing that, do you fancy it? I said" yes, but I don't want a cheap one it's got to be top drawer". We made enquiries and found it was going to cost about £2000, "okay, we can sort it", Bill said" the only problem with a cruise, is that you have to dance, to get the most out of it, but I don't dance." That's okay "we said, we can go to Gladys Southcook on a Friday night, for lessons, its half a crown each, "yes, that's okay" he said.

Bill was a precision engineer, everything had to be spot-on, but he had no sense of rhythm whatsoever. We went for several weeks. After the lesson we would go to the Berni inn, across the road, for a steak supper, which was also half a crown. Teds sister and her husband decided they wanted to go as well, so in the end there were six of us booked on the white funnel line. We were limousined from Harbury Road, to Southampton, and everything was top drawer, fantastic.

We had a wonderful cruise, one of the ports of call was Lisbon, where we met a taxi driver who had a 22 hp Buick, a massive thing. He spent all day driving us round, showing us all the sites. At the end of the day I said "I'm very sorry, but we can't pay". "O my dear "he said," don't worry," send it to me when you get home". Not only did we pay him,. We gave him a very nice tip. Whenever any of our friends were going on a cruise, we gave them his name and phone number and said look him up and say that the bakers have sent you. He got a lot of business out of that day's work.

We had on our table a titled lady, who had a nephew, Nigel, with her. Nigel was an educated idiot, and didn't care about anything or anyone. He was told he had to be down to dinner at eight o'clock, and it was rude to be late, because the waiter would not take the orders until everyone was seated. He strolled in late as usual, and she was very annoyed with him. "I don't know how his mother has brought him up" she said. That was our last night on board, and though we had had our dinner, there was a late-night supper laid on as usual. The captain had decided that as a special treat, the top deck chefs would do fish and chips, served in newspaper, s he went ballistic. My dear, my dear, what is the captain thinking of, this is dreadful. Cruising will never be the same again, from now on, it's going to be for the masses.

We docked in Southampton and again limousined home. The ladies were given pink roses, and the men were given whiskey and cigars. I said to Ted When we got home," that is for us, I don't care if it takes five years six years, that's where we are going again."

A little lad called Johnny Wilcox used to call for Michael in the mornings, to go to school with him. After a couple of mornings, I noticed that he used to watch Michael eat his breakfast, looking very envious. I asked "Have you had your breakfast? "Oh yes", he said, "but not like he's getting". "Would you like some". "Yes please". This went on for a few days. One day I said" what about your mom and dad, where do you live". He replied "I live in a children's home, I'd love to come and stay with you". I said" I don't know if that would be allowed". Anyway, he told me where the home was, and I went round.

I spoke to the man in charge, and asked if it would be possible for John to come and stay with us. He asked if I was sure that's what I wanted. I explained that John and Michael were very close friends, and he seemed a nice lad. So John came to stay. Shortly after this we received a letter from the school, saying that the money people in Doncaster Road had put out for the milkman, was going missing, and they suspected John. I went to the headmaster and said I was sure it wasn't John. But he was fairly sure it was.

We discovered that John came from a family of 13 children, and his grandmother was the most famous pickpocket in Bristol. She had taught him all the different ways to get money. He was now passing this knowledge on to Di and Michael. We had bought him new clothes, new shoes, everything.

Teds auntie died suddenly, and we had to go to the funeral. I asked John if he would like to go to granny Plumpton's with Di and Michael for the day." No" he said," I'd like to go to Portishead". So I gave him some sandwiches, lemonade, and money for the bus, and off he went. When we got home after the funeral Michael was waiting for us." Mum, the police have been on the phone and they want dad to go down to the station. I think John is in trouble". It turned out that he had sold his shoes, and stolen money from some of the caravans on the caravan park. The police were holding us responsible.

When ted Came home we discussed what to do. As Ted said, we had never had anything like this with our own children. And he was now teaching Michael and Diane swear words. We contacted the children's home and told them we couldn't keep him any longer. They came to collect him, but he didn't want to go. "Can I keep the suit, and the watch, and all the things you bought me" he asked." Yes, of course you can". And away he went. That was the last we heard of him for several years, until Diane bumped into him in town one day, he said to her, what a stupid fool he had been. He had been to prison a couple of times and had gone astray. What a better life I could have had with your mum and dad"

At this time we had no transport, so Ted decided we should have bicycles, which we used for visiting the sick. Then he spoke to Joe Johnson, Joe told him that his wife was putting on weight, and they had decided to buy a tandem. Ted said "What about us getting a tandem?" "Yes that sounds good" I said. What I didn't realise was that I was supposed to pedal as well.

Ted tells the story that I didn't lose weight, but he did.

Ted made a sidecar for the tandem, so when we went out Ted would sit up front, me behind, and Michael on a special seat behind me, Diane would sit in the sidecar. We had bought a puppy for the children and when we went out Michael would sit on the back cuddling the puppy.

Ted was very keen to teach the dog tricks. One day I came home from shopping to find Ted jumping back and forth over a broom supported on two low stools. The dog sat watching, thinking, if you think I'm doing that your very mistaken.

We managed to save enough money to buy a small second hand Austin car.

Ted's brother assured him that it was an absolute bargain. He'd be stupid not to buy it. So Ted took all our savings out of the post office and bought it. Ted said "this is wonderful, instead of going by bus to church, we can go in the car".

The following Sunday we were all ready to go, but the car wasn't. Chug, chug, nothing. So we went by bus. On the Monday he bumped into Bill Popes wife. Ted told her about the problems with the car. She said "Well if you can get it up to our house I'm sure Bill will take a look at it". Ted came home and said "We've got to get the car up to Bills". Chug chug, chug chug. So I'm pushing the car, uphill, it suddenly started. There was a bus behind us, so Ted said "Quick, jump on the bus, I'll see you there."

We managed to get to Bills house. He opened the bonnet and looked in.

"Oh, my God" he said, and started pulling bits out of the engine.", Rubbish, and that's rubbish, and this is rubbish," there were bits of engine flying every where. I thought, all we will have in a minute will be four wheels.

Bill said "if I had known how bad it was I wouldn't have asked you to bring it up, it's going to take me a good week to sort it out".

He did sort it, and he wouldn't take a penny for it. That's the sort of chap he was.

We had become quite well known in Bristol. Not just for the healing work, but because Ted could put spiritualism over in a way that people could understand. He was so intellectual that we were invited to take meetings at the twenty one club in Bristol. This was a club for the intellectuals and the hierarchy. It was held once a month in Trelawny Road. The membership was twenty one shillings, but because we did not charge for our lectures, we were allowed to attend any other meetings we fancied.

One week there was a lady due to speak about life on other planets.

I said to Ted, "We must go and listen to that". And we did. She was a very educated lady, and she spoke about life on Venus. She said

"You must understand that there are people on Venus, the difference is that they have green skin and pink vegetation". I thought, oh, really. After she finished the lecture, she said "I'm now going to give clairvoyance. But not in the usual way. I'm going to talk about your past lives". I thought, I don't want to know about my past life thank you.

There was a tiny little old lady present, the medium said "I want to come to you my dear. You were a Princess in a past life. You used to go on the Nile and all the courtiers would bow before you".

I wish I had a camera because that little wizened old lady suddenly preaned, she sat so erect and regal, she became a Princess.

She then went to a young man, "I've got to talk to you because you are terrified of handling money, it's keeping you awake at night, you're sweating, really panicking. The reason is that in a past life you were the keeper of the King's purse and you stupidly ran off with the money. You were caught, and they cut off your head.

That is why the thought of handling peoples money scares you so much".

When they stopped for coffee I made a point of going and talking to the young man. "What did you think of that"? I asked him.

He said, "It was fantastic, I recently joined the Redland tennis club and they have asked me to be treasurer. We are not talking thousands, it's barely hundreds, but the thought of it terrifies me".

Now I know why."

We were invited to the annual dinner. All the Bristol big wigs were there. The Lord Mayor, lord and lady *   *   *, any body that was anybody. When Ted and I dressed for an occasion we really dressed.

We were seated on the top table with the big wigs. The sheriff of Bristol leaned over and said, "By the way Mrs. Baker, what does Mr. Baker do for a living". "Oh," I said, "don't you know". "No" he said, "We have no idea". "He is a flueologist", I replied. "Oh, a flueologist, ", he repeated. He then turned to his wife and said "Darling isn't it wonderful, Mr. Baker is a flueologist". They didn't have a clue that it was a very posh term for chimney sweep.

chapter 5

The day we moved in to 451,(there was accommodation with the shop). Who drove up behind the furniture van? The bailiffs. "You can't take over this shop, all the goods are being repossessed" I sat on the counter and said "Your not taking anything out of this shop, I've just paid for it, and your not taking it". "I'm sorry" they said, "but we've got to". I said if you take anything, you'll have to take me". They went outside and had a con flab. One came back in and said "Sell as much as you can over the weekend, we'll be back Monday. That weekend we had a ball, we were selling big jars of pear drops, licorice allsorts, boxes of chocolates, everything at half a crown a time. There were queues outside, fighting to get in. When the bailiffs came back there was very little left. We have to take it to the pound they told us, but if you want any of it you can come and buy it, we'll make sure you get it. They were brilliant, absolutely marvelous.

Mr. Phillips, who had owned the shop, had two large Alsatian dogs.

They had shredded the doors and the whole place needed complete re decorating. The chaps that worked at B.A.C just up the road, would come in for their papers and sweets etc. Two of these chaps that were regulars came in one morning and asked what I intended to do about decorating the place?. I told them I didn't know. "Well me and my mate could come in after you shut, and work through the night, doing one room at a time". So this is what we did. They did it beautifully.

It took them just over a week to do the whole house, I was thrilled.

I told them that they were wasted at B.A.C., they should set up on their own. They were not too sure about that. I told them to think about it, and if they decided to do it, I would guarantee to pay their mortgage for six months. One of them said he would discuss it with his wife, but the other one said there was no point him asking his wife because she wouldn't entertain it.

The one that took up the offer is now a millionaire in his own right, and would you believe, a few years later started a ladder hire business in competition to me.

Ted and I and four others used to go round on a Friday night and collect the paper money, if you didn't get it on Friday it would be gone.

I called at one house, and while the lady was paying me, there was a baby screaming in the back ground, and she was crying. "What's matter my dear" I asked. "Well" she said "You can hear it, I've got twins. The little girl is fine, but the boy just cries day and night, and every feed he takes, he brings back up. The hospital can't find out what's wrong with him". I said "Would you like me to try and help?"

"What can you do" she asked. "I don't know, but I can try". "Oh yes please, anything". So I called to Ted who was at the next house, and we went in and worked on the baby. When we had finished, I said "I think you will find he'll stop crying now, and he should keep his next feed down".

I could hardly wait to the next morning, to go and see how he was.

"It's marvellous" she said, "He slept all night, and he's kept his morning feed down. Do you know what was wrong with him?"

"Yes" I said," his stomach was twisted"

That was our first paper round healing. The next one was a lady that had stomach cancer, Mrs. Williams. She came to the door one Friday night holding her stomach. "What's the matter," I asked. She explained that she had been diagnosed with this cancer and they didn't think they could do anything for her. She was in a lot of pain. "Would you like me to try and help" I asked. "What can you do". I explained that Ted and I both did healing. "Oh, come in "she said. We worked on her several evenings for about two weeks. Gradually the pain was easing, gradually she started eating, she started getting stronger. At the end of the time she'd been back to the doctors and he could not believe how well she was. She said she was sure that whatever we had done, had cured her. She was a Catholic, and she was going to go to the church and thank God for her recovery. On the way out of the church she met the priest. He said how nice it was to see her out and about and asked her how she was keeping. "Oh father, I'm wonderful, I've had healing and I'm cured of the cancer" "Don't talk so ridiculous" he said, "Who told you Your cured?" "Mr. and Mrs. Baker that do the papers have been giving me healing" she replied. He hit the roof. "You wicked girl "he said, "You must beg God for forgiveness, don't you ever let those people over your door again".

The next Friday when we called, she said she was sorry but she couldn't let us in. "That's O.K." I said we don't need to. She said, "I don't know why the father was so upset, I didn't think I did anything wrong". "No, my dear, you didn't".

The next one was a lady who had erasyphalis, a swelling of the face, very painful. It was Ted that was knocking her door, he called out that he would treat her and for me to carry on collecting. He treated her for quite a while. In the end she was completely cured. Another case was Christopher Booker, a completely normal little boy, until he had the measles vaccine. He couldn't speak properly and was deformed. His mother was convinced it was the injection that caused it. We used to go every Friday night to treat him, and he called us paper man and paper lady. We treated him for years and years.

The next one to mention was Ted Gibson, who lived at 18 Dunmill rd.

Ted, his wife, daughter, son in law and three grandchildren all lived in the same house. Claira, his wife, was disabled. If she wanted to go upstairs, she had to go up on her bottom. One day when I called in her daughter was there, having just come out of hospital after a hysterectomy operation. The hospital had arranged for her to go to Bournemouth, to a convalescent home for two weeks to recover.

"Oh, that's lovely Vi" I said. She said "Yes, but I've got a strange feeling that I will not be coming back". "Don't be silly", I said, "of course you'll be back". She did not come back, she died in the convalescent home.

The weight of looking after them all fell on poor Claira. She wanted to make life as normal as possible for the children. She booked a fortnights caravan holiday in Weymouth for them all. On the Friday night as they were getting ready to go, Claira came in and said, "Ted's in a bad way, can you come and take a look at him?" He was covered in dermatitis, weeping sores all over, it was in his hair, his ears, everywhere.

So we worked on him, "I can't go like this" he said. "No, you can't go like this, but you will be able to go next Saturday and have the second week with them". "I can't see that" he said. The family went off and Ted and I went in every day and worked on him. By the following Friday, it had all gone. He was cured and he went off to Weymouth on the Saturday.

You would have thought there was no way he would be going on holiday.

It was miraculous, thanks to the guides and helpers.

Claira was a wonderful lady, and later on in life I did nurse her when she came into the Haven, a nursing home we had in Bristol

On the evening I was due to give my first clairvoyant demonstration at Surrey House, it was absolutely tipping it down. One of the paper boys had not turned up, so we had to use the spare boy, who was paid one and a half times, what the other boys got. What we didn't know was that he had not told his family how much he was earning. I was just ready to go when his father came storming into the shop, in an absolute rage. He was shouting and bawling and cursing me to heaven. People like you shouldn't be allowed to live, etc, etc. Ted heard this from the back room and as he came through to the shop to sort it out, the man dropped to the floor, dead. Ted told me to go to Surrey House and he would sort everything out. Of course the ambulance and the police came, but I had left by then. I don't remember driving to Surrey hse, I don't remember anything about the clairvoyance or anything, as I was coming down the stairs out of the church, Mr. Gulliver said "Mrs. Baker are you alright". And when he said that, I came back into being me, up until that time I had completely blanked out. Spirit shut it out so that I could deal with the service.

We didn't find out until after, that the boys father thought his son was only getting a pittence.

At this time our church work was really expanding, we were going to Doncaster, Coventry, all over the place. We had a couple of friends that would come in and do the shop while we were away. This went on for quite a while. One day I said to Ted that perhaps we should go in for a different type of business, with the papers, what wasn't sold by mid day was dead. I said I'd thought about a hardware business, but I wasn't sure.

He said "yes, why not, if the nails don't sell this week, so what?" So we then started looking for suitable premises. We found one in Harbury Rd, which is only about half a mile from Southmead Rd. We contacted

Mrs. Bacon, the owner. She was always done up like a band box, as if she was going to a ball or something, immaculately dressed, hair and make up perfect. She assured us it was a thriving business, a gold mine. So I asked to see the accounts. Oh my dear, they are still at the accountants, you know what they are like. "That's O.K I'll call back" I said. When I went back, still no books. "You don't need to see the books, I can tell you we take £90 per week, a third of that is profit. I said to Ted," That's not too bad, you have the sweep business and I've still got the ladders, that's still going on. So we made an offer, which she grabbed with both hands. I have now put the news agents up for sale. A middle aged couple came who were quite sure they wanted to buy, so we made all the arrangements for them to buy and for us to move to Harbury Road. When would you believe, the gentleman had a heart attack and died. We had already put down a deposit on Harbury. So we are stuck. Our solicitor advised us to pull out of the deal, but I didn't want to do that.

We had a phone call from a man called Louie Levi Phillips, who told me that he was buying a chain of shops, but they had to have a certain level of turnover. He came and inspected the books. "Yes that's O.K, I'll purchase it" he said. After he left I said to Ted," There's something funny about this bloke, he comes in a limosine, but his suit is donkeys years old, the seat of his trousers are so shiny. I don't think he is genuine."

I phoned his solicitors, Bobbit's and Bobbit's. "How dare you insinuate our client is not genuine", he said. Mr. phillips was trying to impress me and asked me to go to his offices in White Ladies Road, to finalise the deal.

He sent his limo to collect me and take me there, I was escorted in to the very plush offices, secretaries, receptionist etc. He asked lots of questions,.

What about Cadbury's, what about Wills's, and so on.? I was then taken back home. I discovered much later on that he used to just rent the office for two hours.

Mr. Phillips came to the shop and was telling us about all his grand ideas, he was going to do this and that and the other, you wont recognise it. But, he said "I can't manage all of these shops myself, I'm advertising for managers, they have to put money in. I've got a young family coming back from Nairobi, because they want their three boys educated in England.

Would it be alright if they move rite away, it will only be a couple of days until the deal is finalised?" Ted wasn't too sure, but I thought, poor devils coming back with no where to stay, O.K. Let them move in.

My solicitor, Mr. Elliot, hit the roof. "You fool" he said, "We've had no money from this bloke yet, and I don't think the deals going to go through".

We have now moved in to Harbury Road, with only having paid the deposit. Every thing is in limbo. We then discovered that Levi Phillips is placing orders with Cadbury's, W.D.& H.O.Wills etc in my name. As the shop was still in my name. We then had to find another buyer, which is not easy when you have a family with three children living there.

It was an absolute night mare. I honestly can not remember how we got out of it, but we did.

Mr. Louie Levi Phillips got twelve years imprisonment for fraud.

At the end of our first weeks trading in Harbury Road, we did the accounts and we had taken just £9, not the £90, we had been led to expect. We had a good look at every thing, there were tins of paint that had been there for years, all sorts of things. I said to Ted "it doesn't matter, you have your business, I have mine, and whatever happens to this shop, is any body's business." We got ourselves established and our healing really did take off. We had five teams of healers working on a Thursday.

To provide seating for people waiting we used to put a plank between two chairs covered with a blanket. There would also be people sitting on the stairs leading up to the healing room. We would work in the afternoon, then take a break, before doing the evening session. We had some wonderful experiences there. Jennifer was a little girl who's grandmother came in the shop one day and told me her daughter had had a little girl. The doctors had told her the baby was spina bifida. "Oh, I'm sorry" I said, "but don't worry, ask your daughter to bring the baby in to us for healing". "Our Ruth would never do that" she said. "Give me a fortnight Mrs. Pitt, and your daughter will bring the baby in" I told her. "I don't think she will" she replied. Two weeks later the mother brought Jennifer in. We worked on her for several years. So much so that we became uncle Ted and aunty Edith. Every Thursday she would come for her healing. One Thursday we were working away when the phone went, our son Michael answered it, "Dad, Jennifer is on the phone for you". Ted took the phone, "hello Jennifer, what can I do for you?" "I'm sorry uncle Ted, but I can't come today, I've got a really bad cold" she said. "That's O.K. Darling I'm sure you'll be better next week". "O.K Uncle Ted, loves you lots" and she put the phone down. Shortly after, Ella, Jennifer's aunty came in.

Ted said "I've just been speaking to Jennifer on the phone". "On the phone" she said, with a puzzled look, "Our Ruth hasn't got a phone". "Well she just phoned here, Michael will tell you". That's very strange" Ella said "it was her birthday last week and we bought her a toy plastic phone".

Explain that; she wanted to talk to uncle Ted, and she did.

We had a couple of outstanding successes in Harbury Road, one was a little girl called Valerie, that had leukaemia. when she first came she was about seven years old. The doctors had said there was no cure. She came every Thursday for six months. At the end of this time, the specialist said he couldn't explain it, but she had had a complete cure. The mother was still a bit doubtful, and every three or four months she would bring Her in and asked us to check her over. This went on until she was about 14. That girl is now a healer in her own right.

, We had another patient, called Mr Gulliver, who had a grocery shop in Kingswood Bristol. He was suffering with dermatitis, and because he was selling bread and cakes etc. he was not allowed to work in the shop. The doctors could not do anything for him, and someone suggested that he came to us. We treated him for several weeks, and he also was completely cured, and like Valerie he also wanted to train as a healer to give back what he had been given.

At this time I used to go to Surrey house on Wednesday afternoons. They used to do Thursday evening healing and they said no one would come on the Wednesday. The first afternoon we treated about six people, by the time I finished we would get 20 people coming. Although it was supposed to be an afternoon session, it carried over to Wednesday evenings as well. I would work the afternoon with my lady healers and then Ted would come down with another couple of healers to·do the evening session. At that time we had a man called Dennis Fare that would come in about 7.30. He would say" you've had a long day, you go home and I'll finish up" I thought, how nice of him. There were only a couple of people left to see. One was a lady called Betty blue eyes, she was a very tiny lady, but very attractive. She had really long eyelashes. We used to joke that you had to stand well back, or she would sweep you off your feet. So offt we went, the next we knew, is that the church president had forgotten something in the church, and had gone back. Only to find Mr fair and Betty doing some very unorthodox healing. That was the last time we left Dennis Fair on his own.

I had been treating a man called Mr Blackmore who had the most horrible leg ulcers. He had tried all sorts of cures, and spent a lot of money to no avail. He was recommended to try us. Madge Holford and I treated him for a few weeks and the ulcers dried up. We were getting to the stage of saying you don't need to come any more. This particular day, he sat in the waiting room, and the receptionist came into the treatment room and told me that two young girls had come in, very nervous, didn't know what to expect, and could I treat them next. I thought, there's only Mr Blackmore, I'm sure he won't mind. So I took the girls. I was wrong, Mr Blackmore got to his feet and stormed out, saying to the receptionist, if that's what Mrs Baker thinks, I won't be coming back.

Thursday evening sessions at home were growing, and there was one gentleman that stands out. Arthur Courtney, he was an ex-sergeant major very rigid, a very upright man. He was passing the corner of the road and he was suffering very badly with back pain. He met a lady he knew who had been in for healing. She said "why don't you go in and see the Bakers?" "why what do they do" he asked. She told him about healing. "how much does it cost". "Nothing, it's free, and it might help" she replied. So he came in, and we treated him. Well from then on I think he told the world. From then on Thursday afternoons and evenings were just chock a block. He thought the world of Ted and I. The day he died, I was sat in the evening, and I suddenly felt his presence standing behind me. I phoned Diane, and she told me he had passed away at three o'clock that afternoon.

There was a hardware chain with a shop in Greystone Avenue, and they were looking for other shops in order to expand. They sent a lady around called Dorothy Wren to have a look at our shop and see what she thought about it. They decided that they would rent the shop from us. We were not bothered about the shop, because we had the chimney sweep and the ladder hire business. So they took over. One day Dorothy said," we're not very busy in the shop, would you like me to take bookings for the sweep and the ladder hire"? "Oh, that would be brilliant if you can do that" I said. We became very firm friends. After a while they decided the shop wasn't worth keeping on, but Dorothy stayed on working for us and the ladder hire grew. So much so, that I was able to buy three houses in Redland, Bristol. Which I converted into nine flats. I also bought a house on Southmead Road, number 707. Then I bought a Garrarge on Southmead Road. We were doing extremely well, thank you.

At that time I was letting out the flats, and having a job holding everything together. I employed a chap called Bob Jackson, who would go to the flats once a week clean the windows and empty the ash bins, and do any odd job. One morning I was out delivering ladders, and for some reason Diane was with me. Bob Jackson got hold of me and said you had better get round to 37 Brighton Road." why, what's wrong" I asked. Well, he said" there's something funny going on in the bottom flat". So Diane and I went round. We had a job to get in, and there was a lot of grunting and groaning coming from the front room. I pushed the door open, to find five naked people making love. I chucked them out, in the nude. I drove round to Redland police station and told them what I'd done. "what "they said, you threw five of them out? "yes" I replied." "We could do with you around here" the policeman said.

Flat 21 became vacant, and I put an ad in the paper. A chap phoned and asked about flat, but he said" before we go any further I would like you to know I'm coloured, not just coloured, black cherry blossom coloured". "That's not a problem" I said. So he came and had a look round, and said he would take it. "Don't you want to ask your wife to see it" I asked." No she trust me" he replied, she is one of the senior nurses at Southmead Hospital. They turned out to be the greatest, the cleanest, nicest tenants I ever had. They even lifted the lino and scrubbed the floor before they moved their furniture in. When they left, after quite a long time, the whole street turned out. They were such nice, popular people.

The worst tenants were the so-called white collar workers, those on social were okay.".

707 was an extremely nice house, that I let out to what was supposedly one chap and his mate. I would go every Friday night, no rent, no rent, no rent. This went on for about 18 months. I was absolutely livid, I'm paying the mortgage, the rates, the water, everything. I phoned my solicitor and said" what can I do" He said," absolutely nothing, there's nothing you can do". "Okay" I said, "I'll show you what I can do", He said "go very carefully or you will be in trouble". I went home and phoned a jobbing builder I knew through ladder hire. I asked him to bring some tools and meet me outside 707 Monday morning. We parked just a little down the road, and watched as five people came out of the house." Right" I said.

Front door off, back door off, and all the windows out. Put them in your truck, and disappear. When they came back to the house, they went crazy absolutely crazy. And they phoned the police. In the meantime I'm in the house, throwing all their stuff out into the garden. The policeman said "Madam, I could lock you up for this". "I don't care" I said," I've had no rent for 18 months, are you telling me I can't do anything? "You must put the doors and windows back "he said. "I can't" I replied," the builders gone to the pub, and I've just had a message to say he's had a heart attack". "What are you going to do" the policeman asked. I said" well, I'll have to find another builder, but God knows how long that could take". I Got them out.

At that time I had an empty flat at 37 Brighton Road, and a chap came down from Scotland, called Bill Doherty. He had a look round and agreed to move in. From that day on I never had to worry about those three houses, if there was a tap washer needed replacing, or a door was sticking, whatever, he would deal with it. And he would collect the rents. That was great.

The garage I bought on Southmead Road was on a very small plot. It had been a warehouse for a hardware business and it came with 500 guzzunders (chamber pots for under the bed). I asked our solicitor about building a house on the site. He told us we would never get planning permission. I sold it some years later, and what is on the site now ? a house. We had a receptionist at Harbury Road called John Phillips, he would make a note of the patient's address and telephone number etc, he would then ask, what does your doctor say? is it your kidneys, your liver, your heart, what does he think? I would then do my own diagnosis, and sometimes this did not agree with the doctors. We had a marvellous band of healers, there was Madge Holford and her husband Harold, John and Doreen Keel, Dennis Saxon and Ron Wirret, Jim and Ella Wilcox, and occasionally a trainee healer, coming to learn. One particular night, Ted and I were working on a new patient with a trainee called Fred Donaldson. As we were treating this patient, a control came through to Ted, and was speaking German. I said to the control spirit "It's no good you coming through in German, I don't understand a word you're saying" Fred looked up and said "don't stop him Mrs B, I speak fluent German" when the healing finished, Fred was able to tell us exactly what the guide had said. They didn't want the lady to know what we were treating her for, it was a very personal thing, very personal. How clever the guides were to get that message through. They knew Fred would be able to understand. How wonderful.

Thursday was always busy people would queue up, cars parked in the road, whatever. My job was to stand at the door, and anybody new, I would diagnose what was wrong with them. Also after treatment, I would ask if they felt any better, and if not, I might change healers, and put them with another team, and sometimes this would work.

This particular evening a chap Came to the door, I said good evening Sir, is this your first visit" he said "yes it is". "Well if you would sit down, I will try and diagnose what's wrong". so he sat down. When I diagnose I place one finger on the forehead and another on the back of the head. this puts me right inside the person, I am then drawn to the liver, kidneys, gallstones, whatever. I could find nothing wrong with this man. Eventually I said" I'm very sorry, but I can't find what's wrong with you, you will have to tell me". He said" there's nothing wrong with me, I came to hire a double 23 ladder.

When I saw the queue, I thought, whatever it is they are having, I want some of it. But what I've seen here this evening explains something that happened many years ago. My mother took me to a lady called Mrs Smith. In those days I walked with calipers on my legs. She took me there three times, and then my calipers came off, and I've never had to wear them since. I'm so glad I came" I then took the details for the ladder.

He turned out to be the chief fire officer at Bristol Fire Brigade

Michael was on TV twice. One time he was on with the football finals. With one of the local celebreties, I can't think of his name. Anyway this celebrity said to Michael, "What does the clairvoyant say"? So Michael said "The first goal will be scored in the 35th minute". So the chap anounced that. And the first goal was scored in the 35th minute. And what does the medium say about the final score"? "It will be two all" which it was.

Michael got a lot of publicity, and also he was asked to go on the radio, and television. With Diana Dors, Diana was talking to him about his work and asked him what his parents did. So Michael said "They are both healers, they work in the church's and they live in Bristol." "That's very interesting" she said. "You'd better give out the telephone number, then anybody who needs to contact them can do so". So Michael gave it, and from that we had Craig Randall, his father rang up and that was how we start with Craig. And from then on, for the next five years, we went to visit him every Saturday afternoon without missing. At one time, when he was a little better, and we had Wick house, we were able to have him for a fortnight, in order to allow his family, to have a much-needed holiday. It was a very sad case, because gradually, as the years went on, we could see that we were not going to win this one.

All we could do, was try making him as comfortable as we could. But it was lovely because on Saturday afternoon, when we went to visit him, he would roll his eyes, and then a lovely smile would come across his mouth. He was obviously very pleased to see us, we had a great rapport with him. Unfortunateley, after five years, we did lose him. If we did have a holiday or anything, we would have other healers, go to visit him on the Saturday afternoon so that he wasn't left without somebody going to him.

Michael phoned me up after his interview with Diana Dors and he said "She does not know it, but she will be in the spirit world in three months".

And it was three months later that she died of cancer. She had no knowledge of it when Michael made the prediction.

One morning, as I was loading the ladders on the truck, and Ted was getting ready to go and do the chimneys. Chan came through, "Go to 16 Ridgeway Road, go now," he's shouting in my ear," Go now". I said to Ted, "I can't stop I've got to go. I didn't know what I was going to find. I drove across Bristol like a madman. I got to Ridgeway Road, I knew the house because I had been healing the man and his wife. Instead of going to the front door, I raced straight round to the back. I banged the door open. She was in the kitchen, with her head in the gas oven, with her head on a pillow. He was sat next to her holding her hand. I pulled her out of the oven and turned the gas off. I opened all the doors and windows, He said "Mrs Baker, what are you going to do"? I said "strictly speaking, I should be on the telephone to the police. This is assisted suicide. But I shan't be doing that. He said "Well, what are you going to do?" I said, get a blanket. I wrapped her in the blanket, she was only a tiny little soul. I put her in the cab Of the truck and drove her back to Harbury Road. He followed in the car. (This was another time that Di lost her bedroom. Quite often she would come home at midnight, to find someone in her bedroom). She was a lady that suffered very badly with head pains, none of the doctors or consultants she had seen could do anything about it. What thrilled me was that one day the vicar from Fishponds came to see her. He sat talking to her in the lounge. When he got up to go, he said "I cannot explain it, but there is a wonderful Holy feeling in this room. I've never felt anything like this outside of the church. She eventually got much better and went home.

We were quite a few years in Harbury Road. I decided to sell ladder hire. I sold it for £2000, to a man called Robert. He thought it would be a doddle. He would turn up in a collar and tie and suit, then change into overalls to do what ever deliveries and collections, and then change back into his suit to go home. If I got a call at five or six o'clock at night for a ladder, I didn't put it off to the next day. I would go and do it. This particular day, I took an order for a ladder, which was on his way home, he lived at Winterbourne. When he came in from the deliveries, I said "I have just taken an order, you can drop it off on your way home". "Certainly not, I shan't be doing that until tomorrow morning". He said. I said "Surely it would be sensible to do it now". "I don't go home in overalls, I go home in a car" he said. And so I thought, right, The next day when he came in we were sat talking and I said, "You're fed up with this business, aren't you? "Yes, frankly I am, I don't like getting my hands dirty for a start," he replied. I said," Well, I'll tell you what, I'll buy it back off you. But you will have to wait for the money, it will take me twelve months to do it. I will pay you so much a month, for 12 months. He said "Would you do that?" I said, "Yes, I would."

I remember, I did get an order one night, about 1130. I was in bed, when the phone went, and this chap Said he wanted a ladder. Quick as a flash, I said "Did you want it now Sir, or can it wait until the morning. (I was being sarcastic). While I had ladder hire, I'm also doing funerals and taking services etc.

I had to take a funeral service for a man in Bishopfort Road, just round the corner from Harbury Road. I'm not sure if it was 9 AM or 930. I like to go and talk to the family beforehand, and find out a bit about the person. So I can make the service a bit more personal. On the day of the funeral, Dorothy Wren, who was the receptionist to ladder hire, had taken a booking for 10 o'clock. I said to Ted, "I am not going to have time to come home and change, so I will put my overalls on, and put my big black astrakhan coat on. With my Bible, and all the bits, they wouldn't know what was underneath". I will take the service, than go around to deliver the ladder, no problem. I went round to Bishopsfort Road, and she came to the door saying, "What are you doing here Mrs B?" I said," I've come to take the service". "But my dear, they've already gone". "Oh," I said, "I was going to get a lift with them". So I jumped back in the truck and raced down to Canford. At the cemetery there is a big long drive, all the way up the drive there are weeping willow trees, hanging over. Because I had rushed out I had not tied the ladders on properly. I stopped at the gate and thought, shall I leave the truck here and run up the drive. That is not very ladylike. I will drive up. As I'm going up the drive, ladders are going bump, bump, bump, off the back of the truck. When I got to the door, the funeral director said, "Don't worry Mrs B, only you and I know what has happened. By the time you come out the ladders will be neatly tied on the wagon, and nobody will be any the wiser.

Another time I was coming out of Canford, the snow was about 6 feet deep, and we were stopped by a funeral coming in. The funeral director came to our funeral director and said, "Do you think your vicar would stay and take another service". "I don't know" he said, "I will ask her, it's a lady". "We don't mind who it is, our vicar Is snowed in, and cannot make it" "That's okay" I said. "I'll do it". I got out, but I didn't have any time to talk to anybody. All I knew was that it was a man, in his 90s, and his name. I stood up to take that service, and I'm talking about the sea, and the oceans. Coming into harbour, how the tides move us this way, and that way, but in the end, we all come into the same harbour. A chap came up to me afterwards, and said "That was wonderful. That was my father, and he was an Admiral, he's been at sea all his life. You couldn't have known anything about that. It all just fitted in so perfectly".

, There was a very old crematorium in Bristol called Arnos Vale. In those days there was nothing electrical. Everything was hand driven. One day I was taking the funeral service, and Sam was sat by the plinth, waiting to wind down the Coffin. I would wait till the people bowed their heads in prayer, then I would give Sam the nod, to start winding. I did the service, and then we were saying the Lord's prayer, everyone had their head bowed. So I am nodding to Sam, who is well into his 70s, to start winding. But Sam had nodded off. The funeral director was very quick, and gave Sam a shake. We just managed to get the Coffin down before the people raised their eyes.

Ted sold chimney sweeps, and took over ladder hire. Looking in the evening Post on Friday night, I saw a hotel for sale. Nine bedrooms, in Stokes Croft Bristol, just off the centre. We went with a friend, Roy Silverdale, to have a look. The asking price was £22,000. It had been running since 1946. We looked at the books and said, okay we will buy it. It was a commercial hotel, doing bed and breakfast.

We went home and phoned Mr Griffiths our solicitor, "Can we meet you in your office 9 AM tomorrow". "Yes, what are you buying now" he asked. "A hotel" I replied. "Okay, bring the paperwork down". We were going on holiday, the following Monday. So on the Sunday, I went to the accountants at Henbury, with all the documents. That was all fine. Monday morning I went to the bank, and withdrew the money, then to the solicitors to collect the deeds and hand over the money. Then a mad dash to Cardiff airport, to catch our flight to Majorca. We ended up running down the tarmac, just in time to catch the flight. I sat down and said to Ted" what have I done"? He said "you have just bought the Arches Hotel,

"We are off for two weeks in Majorca, and your opening 1 January. On our return we moved into the hotel, there was like a piece on the back that we had made into a sort of bungalow. When we took over on 1 January, we had three staff, Jackie, Mary, and Betty. I hate artificial flowers and everywhere I looked there they were. I asked Mary "have you got a nice big dustbin"? why" she asked. "Just follow me" I said. We went round and binned every flower. We then went round inspecting the rooms. Only to discover that one of the beds, was propped up with bricks. We did a complete make over. New beds, new furniture, etc. It was a well supported hotel. Used mainly by commercial travellers and sales reps of all kinds. They were a really good bunch. We had some really good laughs with them and became very friendly.

We were still doing healing at Harbury Road, and Ted was still running ladder hire. Diane met and married a chap from Thornbury, Mick Pearce. Who drove an aggregate lorry.

The Arches was a lovely Hotel and business was booming. I got a phone call from a lady who asked, would it be possible to take a couple with two children for a month or two?. I can assure you that the bill will be paid. I had a word the Ted, and we agreed to give it a try.

I used to go to Nerdin and peacocks cash and carry, in Avonmouth, for the hotel supplies. But would usually forget something. There was a little warehouse just up the road, run by two chaps, Ivor and Ron. One Friday I went in, and Ron was sat with his head in his hands. I said "What's the matter Ron ". "Oh, Mrs B, the landlord just came in and trebled our rent, from £30-£90. There's no way we can pay that, we will have to get out". "Well what will you do" I asked. "I don't know, I have no idea". He said. "Well, you will have to come and work for me" I said. "Doing what" he asked. "I don't know, but we will find something, I'm sure". He was a proud man, and didn't like the idea. He wrote 47 letters to different firms seeking work and not one replied. And so it went on. I said "Ron, you will have to come and work for me. Can you cook bacon and eggs." "Yes, I can do that" he said. "Good, start Monday". And he did. He worked for me for several years, in different ventures. He turned out to be a marvellous chef.

I asked him one day, what had changed his mind about working for me. He pulled a letter out of his wallet and said that he had written to a psychic lady in the newspaper. She had written back, you are going to have a complete change of life, you will be very happy in your new work. Where ever it is, you must look for this sign, and she had drawn three Arches. Our hotel is called the Arches because there are three Arches going over the road.

We had a problem with people leaving, without paying. This had to stop. We decided that they must pay on arrival. One night a chap came in and said his mother was in hospital dying. He had come down from Manchester, he had no identity, no money, nothing. I said "I'm sorry, no". "You're denying me a bed, and my mother is dying" he said. I said "Sorry, no", I went off into the kitchen and thought, what a heartless cow. What have I stooped to. Ted said "you made the rules, you must stick to them". The following morning the lady from the hotel across the road came over. "Did you have a man come in here last night, whose mother was dying" she asked. "Yes" "Well he's gone, and he's taken the TV the duvet and drinks" she said. Ted said "there you are"

At one time, we were absolutely full up. Two Italian ships officers came in. I tried to explain we were full but they did not understand, Ted walked in, and explained in perfect Italian. They thanked him, picked up their cases, and left.

We had a couple who came up from Cornwall. They were being sent on government business to Bristol. The bill had to be sent to Inland Revenue. After the first week, he came down and said that he was being transferred to London, but his wife would be staying on. He was a very smart and well mannered, a respectable bloke. He was away for nearly a month. When he came back, he was a changed man.

I could not believe it was the same bloke. He looked so ill. His nerves had gone, he was in a terrible state. "What ever happened in London", I asked. He said, "I'm not supposed to speak about it, but I am no longer a tax inspector. I was a top man for the area. But I no longer work for Inland Revenue. When I went to London they gave me three big companies in Bristol to investigate. One of these was Berni Inns. What I found, I reported back to Inland Revenue. I was told to go away, and forget what I had found. I could not believe what they said. I gave in my resignation. Like all my colleagues, I took an oath that black is black, and white is white, there is no grey area.

The lady that had phoned up earlier, asking if we would take a family, phoned again. Could we take another family? I wondered what was going on. Eventually she came clean and said she was social services. They eventually filled the Hotel. I could have stayed there and become very rich, they just threw money at us, via these disgusting families. I got to the point I couldn't take any more. We had the fall outs, the dropouts the drug addicts, the drunks the absolute dregs of society. The money was brilliant, you could ask whatever you wanted. Every now and again she would come round and say "If you were to halve that dining room you could take another family. If you got rid of the dining room, you could take another two families". I said to Ted, "I can't go on with this, this is not our sort of life".

The most awful thing, was the way parents treated their children. One particular family had three children, and were due to be rehoused in a months time. The father came into the kitchen one morning and said, "Mr Baker, would you stop giving our children breakfast. My wife and I will still have it, but don't give it to the children, when we move into our own place next month, they will not be getting breakfast". Ted was horrified, so what did he do? He would take the children into the garden and feed them. And tell them not to tell their parents. We had some very difficult people to deal with. One was a chap called Mr Reece, he was a VAT tax inspector, and had been thrown out of his house late one afternoon. Social phoned and said, "I know you've just got a family room vacant, we want to put Mr Reece in, with his wife and two children. They are on the way now, we have paid for a taxi for them. He arrived, all tarted up, and he had got a cat with him. "I'm sorry" I said. "We don't take animals". "O my dear" he said. "What am I going to do?" I said, "Well, you will have to put it in a cattery ". "It's too late now, what can I do". "Okay, Mr Reece, one night, then it must go" I replied. "Yes, I shall get rid of it tomorrow". I never thought any more about it. A couple of days later, one of my staff came in and asked if I had been up to room nine. "No, why" I asked. She said "You had better come up". When we went in, there was mummy cat, with three kittens, sitting on the bed. I went loopy.

I wanted to find a different way of life, perhaps caring for those who really needed caring for. I told Ted that we were going to live on the Downs, I did not know where, but it would be on Bristol Downs. I started driving round looking for a house. There was one I found, but I didn't think we could afford it.

We went away on a cruise, as always happens, I met someone in need of healing. I've never yet had a cruise without getting involved in healing. While we were away my sister was standing in for us. On our return I was more determined than ever to escape from what we were doing. I went to an estate agents in the centre, and right in the middle of the window, was the Haven. I enquired about it, and was told that at the moment it was divided into flats. The asking price was £150,000, a lot of money in the 1960s. I went and had a look, I knew instantly that it was going to be mine. I went back to the agents and said I wanted to buy it. He told me that we would have to be quick, because the society for the deaf were after it. They were waiting on a decision from their committee. He suggested if we offered an extra £2000, we would get it. I went back and told Ted, and we decided we were going to sell the Arches. To sell a business, you have to advertise it. On the Saturday afternoon, I was sat in the office writing an advert to put in the newspaper. My guide, Chan, came through and said "Missy, no advertise". "we can not sell the Hotel without advertising it". "Missy, no advertise" he repeated. So I put the pen down. On the Sunday we were taking the service at Cairns Road Church. After the service, Mrs Cox came up to me, and said her son wanted to go into business. Could he come and have a word with me? I explained that I was very busy, but if he could come down at 9 PM I would see him. His wife was a nurse, and they were thinking of a nursing home or a bed and breakfast, they didn't really know what. "I said "This is up for sale". "Oh, really, can I have a look" he asked. He had a look round, and looked at the books, and said "I want to buy it" "Okay, you will have to get a mortgage sorted out" I said. "That will not be necessary" he replied. "I'm the manager of Lloyds bank". That is how we sold the Arches. Chan had been right.

We then set about moving to the Haven. It was in a very prestigious part of Bristol, every body was frightfully, awfully, so I became frightfully, awfully, as well. When in Rome, etc. I bought all the carpets and furniture top drawer, because we were going to have top drawer people. I had to get planning permission for change of use. Two days before the planning meeting, I heard that the neighbours had got a petition up against it. I thought, oh my God, what am I going to do? I spent all this money, and if we don't get planning? Chan said "Go and talk to Mr Woodgate, the butcher". So I went in and said to him "I'm cheesed off, I've just heard the neighbours have got a petition against me opening a nursing home or a residential home, and we've just spent the Earth doing it up". "O my dear, that's terrible", he said. I said "Yes, but the governor of Horfield prison has been to see me, and said, if we don't get planning permission, he would like it as a rehabilitation centre for prisoners on their release. I don't really want to do that, but I will have no choice. Please don't say anything to anyone will you". "Certainly not" he said.

Before I got home, the curtains were twitching. People were coming up to me saying, we do hope you get permission, we don't want those prisoners, do we?. On the Friday morning I went to the planning meeting. The chairman stood up and said there was an application for 27 Downs Park Road to be opened as a nursing home. But I believe there are some objections, who is objecting?. Not one person objected.

Ted loved the Haven, it had very large gardens. The house was on three floors and we had to work out how to get patients up and down. I phoned stannah lifts, and they sent a man called Mr Abel. I explained that I wanted an internal lift. That's not possible, he assured me. You will have to have a stairlift. That's £2700, we can fit it next week. When the engineer came to fit it, he asked why we had not had a passenger lift. I explained Mr Abel said it was impossible. The engineer explored the building, and came back to say that we could have a passenger lift for four people, at a cost of £7000. I had spent 2700 that I need not have done, because Mr Abel just wasn't able. The accommodation was absolutely beautiful. The patients that were mobile would eat in the dining room. One day they asked if they could speak to me. Would you mind very much if we could have our dinner at lunchtime, instead of the evening?. That suited me fine, because in the evening I could just do sandwiches and cakes or something. It made life a lot easier for the kitchen staff. I always say that your success depends on your staff. Ron, who had come with us from the Arches, would always go that extra mile. One day, in the middle of August with the sun baking down, I went in the kitchen and he was making onion soup. "Ron" I said, We haven't got onion soup on the menu". "I know" he replied, "but Mr Lovell is very poorly, and he loves onion soup". Another time, it was in December, he was chopping strawberries. Very hard to come by at that time of year. "Mrs Sherman is very poorly, we are trying to get her to eat. So I'm doing her strawberries and cream". That is why we were so successful, our staff would fall over backwards for the patients.

I remember one day, Mrs Sherman was in a real state. "I don't know what I'm going to do" she said. "That Doctor has stopped my pills. I've been on them for years. what can I do"? I said "Don't worry my dear, I will get you some pills that will replace the ones the doctor has stopped, but you must not tell anybody. They would close us down. Come into the kitchen at 10 AM and see either me or Ron, and we will give you a pill. I went out and bought some tiny peppermint sweets. And every morning, at 10 o'clock, I would give her one. "Oh, Mrs B, you won't believe it. I've never felt so well, I'm so glad that Doctor stop those pills.

Another patient, Mrs Brown, thought that everybody's teeth ought to go into a big bowl at night. One night, when everyone was asleep, she crept into all the rooms and put the teeth in a big bowl. How she got away with it, I do not know, because we had night staff on. The following morning you can imagine what happened. One lady was as poor as a church mouse but would act very lahdedah, matron took her breakfast tray in and she said "I don't understand it. I have had these teeth 30 years, and I have never had any trouble before".

Another patient was an ex-Bluebell girl, who after she retired, had had an accident involving a bus, and had lost a leg. Her false leg was kept by her bed. One day Sandy came down and said, "I think Grace Goody has got whiskey in her room" "I don't think so" I replied. She said, "I'm telling you, there is whiskey in the room, I can smell it". We searched everywhere, we did find it eventually, hidden in the false leg.

We also had Mr Rees, a top orthodontist. Who would sit in the lounge and say, "If you brought me my tools, I could sort all their teeth problems. We had one lady, Miss Jenkins, who arrived in tatters. You could shoot peas through her underwear. A firm of solicitors phoned, and said the bill must be sent to them for payment. The girls would come down and say, she's got no clothes, she's got no this, she's got no that, and they started running coffee mornings to get enough money to go to Marks and Spencers and buy her some underwear. I said to Sandy "She might be in rags, but that lady, is a lady". "No, I don't think so" she said. The solicitors would always query the bill. Are you sure she had two bottles orange juice etc. When she died, it turned out that she was Lady Georgina Jenkins. A cousin to the Queen, and she owned half of Tetbury and Thornbury. She owned so much property, it just wasn't true. Her funeral was attended by several royals, as well as numerous ladies and Lords.

We also had Mr Watts, a multi-millionaire and owner of Watts tyres, Watts cars, etc. When he came, he brought his own nurse with him, al though we provided nursing care, he also had his own. At times he would escape from her, and would come down in the nude, or another time he would come down wearing two lots of everything.

Dr Nurse was another, she had been a doctor in St Pauls Bristol. She lost six brothers in the first world war. She was a spinster. She would come into my office and say, "I have told them not to let any more patients in tonight. I have just been in the waiting room and there are another 10 patients. I'm going out to dinner, they will have to send them home. I cannot cope. "That's all right, I'll help you" I would say. We used to hold garden parties, and at Christmas we would have a pantomime, put on by the staff.

The Haven

This is about a little girl that fell in the playground at school. It was three o'clock in the afternoon, and they rushed her to hospital to discovere that she's got a tumour on the brain, and take her in to operate on immediately. So mother and father are sent for and they go to the hospital. The child is put into intensive care. So they stay with her until about 8-30, the theater nurse said" there is no point in you staying, she's in intensive care, she's got the best care possible. Go home and relax and come back in the morning".

So they went to walk home, and while walking down Gloucester Road, in Bristol. She says she's got a terrible headache, she said, "I could really do with some aspirins". They look across the road and see the chemist shop light on. So they go over and knock the door. And so the chemist comes out, and it turns out to be a man called Mr chant, that I have been treating for years. They relayed the story of the child having fallen, and in intensive care. He said," Well, you need more than aspirin my dear, you need to get hold of the Bakers. They are healers", he said. "Go to them, go to them now". So he gave them the address, and they came across to Southmead, by which time it's about 11 o'clock and we are both in bed, the door bell is ringing. We go down and they relayed the story. I shouted to Ted, "quick, we are off to Frenchey hospital". He jumped in to his clothes and we go to the hospital. Now you cannot get into intensive care unless you are a relation. Who comes to the door of intensive care?, one of my senior nurses. "Oh", she said, "My God, Mrs Baker, I've been praying for you to come, they said that the cut it so fine they are afraid she might go blind". "O.K. we will treat her". From then on we went in every day and every night to treat her, and by the end of the week she moved out of intensive care, and no sign of being blind. We went on treating her and she became fully restored.

Another story on top of that, because we then discovered that she was a niece of Ann Penn. Ann Penn was a lady who had belonged to Surrey house church before passing. You can imagine, the child gets this accident, Ann Penn gets the message in the spirit world, got to get the Bakers to her, and that's how that story was complete.

When we were almost finished decorating the Haven, a taxi drew up, and the front doorbell rang, and this lady got out, with a suitcase. She said "You are opening this as a residential and nursing homes arn't you"? "Yes we are". "Right, I'm moving in" "I'm sorry" I said "but we are not ready yet". "You heard me, I'm moving in, As each room is completed, I will move in to it, until I find the one I want", and she did. That was Mable.

We did do a safari holiday, we went to Nairobi. We met at Victoria station, and there are 12 people going on this people carrier, we were driven off to the airport, but it's a foggy night and we can't fly, so we had to stay overnight. And left the next day, we eventualy get to Nairobi and get to the hotel. In the party there are twelve people, I've got this awful knack of naming people. There was Gert and Dais, Three Musketeers, Three Musketeers were the television producer Tony Bowring, a hotel owner who had two hotels in Malta, and a floozy with them. One night she would be in one cabin and the next night the other cabin. We had people from Manchester, who owned a factory making curtains and things and then there was the maiden aunts, terribly excited because they were going on Safari. And then we had Tweedle Dum and Tweedle Dee, they were man and wife and both very large.

He was up at the front in reception, demanding the best rooms. I didn't say anything, and we were all allocated our rooms.

The next day we went on safari, spent all day driving round and did'nt see any animals. Ted said we should have gone to Longleat, there are more animals there. They assured us that we would see more animals the following day because we were moving deeper into the park. And of course we did, we saw elephants, hyenas and every thing.

At night we used to stay in a different hotel for dinner, but you would always be by a watering hole, and watch the animals come down, it was fantastic to see. The Lions would come down first, father lion, mother lion and baby lions. They would go and then the elephants would come and then the giraffs. A moving panorama, simply a wonderful experience. Every night we would have dinner in the hotel, sleep there, and next day go on further into Safari. One time they took us to a little village which was just outside the park, and the top man, the headman, did'nt want to let us in until we paid. So we paid and went in, there were millions and millions of flies. The people came out to see us and the flies were all over the babies, it was horrible, absolutely horrible. I said "How on earth do they manage to sleep at night, with these flies on them? He said, "oh it's no problem, because at night we bring the cows in, and the flies go on the cows.

It took two days to get the flies out of the car. The holiday went on and Tony, the television producer, told the two maiden aunts that Ted and I were Lord and Lady Baker, travelling incogneto, and they didn't have to tell any body who we were. Every night we dined in the hotels at our own tables, but the last night he said how do you feel about making an entrance? "Oh trust me, I can make an entrance" I replied. So he went to see the maitre de and said we have an illustrious couple dining today and every thing must be just right. So we make an entrance, I've got my black on and we swept into the restaurant. We sat down for our meal and the two maiden aunts look across at Ted, and she said "Lord Baker, when did you get knighted, I didn't realise?" "Oh yes, it was for services to the trade union" he replied.

One of the nights when we got to the hotel, and Tweedledum and tweedledee were in the front, pushing as always, I was about to say that enough is enough. We have all payed the same money, and were all entitled to the same treatment. As I'm about to open my mouth, somebody put their hand in front of my mouth. I thought, I'm not meant to say anything. What I didn't know, and discovered after, his wife was terminaly ill with cancer, and he was spending all his life savings taking her on this trip.

At the end of the evening, the man from Malta, said "I always like to give gifts to people I've shared some time with,. so we will have special souvenirs from him. Then I said to Tony "It's time you told them were not really Lord and Lady Baker". "Oh, my God, you can't do that. It would ruin their holiday. They simply cannot wait to get back to tell the people at the tennis club who they shared their holiday with.

Ted set off one morning, and said to me "This customer, the name is Fairchild?". "Yes thats right" I replied. "Thats funny, I was with a chap called Fairchild in the navy, he was killed". So he went off to see this lady and sweep the chimney. He was talking to her about her son, when he said "He's here, he is standing here telling me, to tell you, that he is alright". She said "What proof have you got, what proof have you"., So Ted said, "he's telling me, to tell you to go and get the locket that he bought for you before he went back to sea the last time". So she went upstairs and got the locket.

We did a cruise and went everywhere, and finished at one point in New Zealand, where I've got family, and wanted to meet with them because they emigrated after the First World War. We were coming from the airport and Ted said to the taxi driver" do you happen to know where there's a spiritualist church". "Yes I know one, my wife goes every Sunday". We were staying at the White Heron hotel and Ted said "could you please pick us up and take us to the church on Sunday"? So Sunday came and he picked us up. When we got there she said "Oh, your strangers", she said, "Your both mediums arn't you, where do you come from?". Bristol, England," we replied. "Who taught you" she asked. "Ernie Oaten" I told her. She then asked if we would take the service next Sunday? Which we agreed to.

She told us the most remarkable story, and the story was that they had a man in the church who was a feeler, and not a healer, and they had to tell him to go. He took the church to court for defermation of character, and the church lost. It cost the church £6000, so obviously he moved from the North Island and went to the South Island, and the same thing happened. He was working in a church there, and they had to do the same. so it broke the church in half, because there was a court case, and this time he lost. What they didn't know, if the church ever got split, broken up, the lady who had left it, said that the money had to be split between three other denominations. One was the Salvation Army, one was cruelty to animals, and the third was to another spiritualist church. We are now sending you £6000. So they got their money back.

The self employed used to meet at The Haven, to discuss policy, and one night it was freezing, the fog was thick, instead of the usual 20 or 30 people there was only about 14 managed to make it, because they used to come from Salisbury, Bath, what have you. They decided, instead of having a committee meeting, to discuss how they started in business. Because they were all in different trades and so forth. There was one chap there who said that when he started in business he used to go round door to door selling lemonade.

He realised that the old ladies used to use a lot of fire wood to light their fires. He decided that Mr Davies lemonade crates would chop very nicely into little bundles of fire wood. So he had a double business going. He had the lemonade and the fire wood. It all came to a sudden end because unfortunately the saw that they were using chopped off his mates fingers. Unfortunately it was the end of his fire lighting business.

Another chap said when he was young he thought it's the simple ideas that make money, something stupid. He had a grandmother whos teeth were always black, could he do something about it. So he got some acid and some other stuff and mixed it together. When she had gone to bed that night he took her teeth and put them in the solution. In the morning, what happened? the teeth had all fallen off the plate. He certainly was not the favourite grandson.

The Haven was an extremely successful business, and we were privileged to have the top people in society. We allways had a full house, we always had a waiting list, There were about 60 names on the waiting list. It meant that if we did get a death, we were able to ring the next person on the waiting list and the room was immediately taken. Whilst we were there I became interested in a man called Norman Small, who started the Self Employed Federation in England. He started it because he had heard of the people in Belgium, who were complaining that their government was not giving them enough support. They said they were the lifes blood of the country, and they needed help. So to get a response, they decided one weekend, every self employed person would stop working, and during the next 24 hours the country was on its head.

After the weekend the government decided to listen to these little people, and arranged to give them bank loans, if they could prove that they would employ two or three more people. And this got Belgium off the back foot, because at the time they were struggling.

Norman Small decided that in England a similar thing should happen. He was an ex army major. When he came back from the army he could only find work going round the little shops selling small items, and he was determined that he would get this idea of all these small businesses coming together. He went the length and breadth of the country, Birmingham, Liverpool, Bristol, He announced that on the Sunday afternoon there would be a meeting for everyone that was self employed, in the Grand Hotel, Bristol. For once in our lives we decided that we would go. You couldn't get into The Grand Hotel, there were hundreds of people. There were fishmongers, greengrocers, butchers there were solicitors, every walk of life represented there. We were in the hall of the hotel and Norman Small said what we need is a committee, and some where to hold meetings. Whos hand went up? and where was the first committe meeting,? in the Arches Hotel.

I am telling you this story because of what went on from there. It was decided that to get things done in the world, instead of being on the outside of different departments, we had to be on the inside. So they drew up a list of things people should be set to do. They sent some to become politicians, some to become part of local councils, some to become part of the jury system, and these people were told to go and get themselves elected, so they could work from the inside, instead of from the outside. I was sent to become a magistrate, but when they asked me what religiouse flavour I was, I said "spiritualist". "I'm sorry," it was a no, no. So I did not become a magistrate.

I am only telling you this story because at one time in the Haven we had a lady called Mrs. Rich. She had been with us for about five years. She loved her room, loved the haven, loved everything about it, but she became ill. Social Services decided that because she was deteriorating she should be moved to another nursing home. The relatives said "there is no way we want her moved. Mrs baker has always employed top quality staff and we are more than happy the way mum is being looked after, we don't want her moved." Social services said," we are going to move her". It is August, and I am desperate. Mrs Rich is crying. The relatives are there, and I thought, what can I do? Because it was august most of the Bristol committe are away on holiday. I happened to know that most of the Bath committe were still in situ. So I phoned Bath, and explained the problem. They said Mrs. B don't worry, if you have any problems at all, we will come over and barricade the place. We will make sure Mrs. Rich does not get moved. It's the only time in my life that I was grateful for belonging to any sort of society, they gave me such strength. Sufice to say Mrs Rich did not leave The Haven, and stayed with us until she passed.

The Haven was so popular and it was obvious that we needed a bigger place. I have a habit of reading houses for sale ads. We are going on holiday to Malta for a fortnight, it's on the Thursday evening, and I read Wick House is up for sale. Wick House belonged to social services, and it's been a Playschool, and haven for children in need. I told Ted that it was for sale and I'm going to buy it. I telephoned the agents, and I said "Is it possible for me and my secretary to come and have a look". "Certainly".

So Dorothy Wren, a dear friend of mine as well as my secretary came with me. The Matron is very disconcerting, and didn't really want to show us round. I said "Don't show anyone else round, I'm buying it". I phoned the solicitor, Mr. Brisly and said "I'm going on holiday at the weekend and I want to buy Wick House" I gave him the details of the estate agents and said "could you confirm to make sure that it is mine when I come back".

So I left Dorothy Wren with a cheque to make sure it didn't go anywhere, I am paying £150,000.

We have hassle because when we came back from holiday, social services are still getting stuff out. Now would you believe it is summer, and they had the central heating on for 24 hours a day?, that's social services. Down in the cellar there were stacks and stacks of everything. There were beds,b edding heaters, stoves everything. I asked them if I could buy some of these items, because obviously setting up as a nursing home I was going to need stuff. "Certainly not" they said. "We shall have wagons coming in and we shall clear the cellar" "Where is it going"? "Its's going on the tip" or so they said. I didn't believe it.

These cellars were linked to the Reformation, because the monks and the nuns used to be in that house and to escape persecution, tunnels which go right down into the centre of Bristol. And they are still there today. We also discovered that in the cellar we have somebody called Fred. When you went down in the morning you had to say" good morning Fred" because if you didn't say "good morning" to Fred, he would turn the lights off. When you said "Good morning Fred" the lights would come back on.

Wick House was again very successful, with a waiting list and people from all over the country, not many from Bristol. We had 44 rooms. To open Wick House, I have to have a matron, with all the senior qualifications. Ted and I had gone over with our paintbrushes, any colour you like as long as it is Magnolia. Between taking services, preparing rooms, now we have to have a licence from social services and from NHS. And of course they tell me what qualifications are needed in this senior position. I am desperate to get this matron, and I don't seem to be getting on very well. I'm ready to open, so I'm thinking, what can we do. So I'm asking Chan, I need help. Chan said "in half hour the phone will ring" he said, "a lady will be talking to you from the freemantle, hospital, in Newcastle. You will know that she is the right one by her initials". (She was Valerie Evelyn Smith. Sandy was Violette Evelyn Stanley). You Will know her because she will have the same initials as the matron here"., When Chan tells you something, you just listen. Half an hour later the phone rings, "I'm speaking to you from the Fremantle Hospital, I understand you're wanting to open Wick House as a nursing home. my qualifications are pop pop pop pop pop, I said "Hang on a minute, can you tell me your initials". How I managed not to say come down, you've got the job, I don't know. But I did say that it's rather urgent, can you please come as soon as possible, if necessary, fly down. Now what I was not prepared for, and it was a bit of a shock, she was Butch and was she butch. The short back and sides, arms like an navvy. Her qualifications and the way she ran Wick House could not be faulted. The only downside, and it didn't happen until a few years after, when we took on and a junior nurse and she became the partner of Valerie Smith. Unfortunately from there on things did not go quite so well. It took me a long time to realise what was happening.

We had some wonderful, wonderful times. The grounds were beautiful, and we used to have garden parties. On this particular day I had arranged for patients relatives to come to a garden party, and I was expecting 40-50 people. That was okay, Ron Parnell was in the kitchen doing scones with jam and cream. All of a sudden there's a band, Scouts are marching, Girl Guides are marching, Brownies are marching, some idiot had arranged for the guides and scouts the same-day I arranged the garden party. To say the least, it was a beautiful day, an absolutely wonderful day and the patients loved it. They all went to bed very tired. Added to that, we were exhausted.

<u>Wick House</u>

Wick House was very successful but we decided it was going to have to be sold because of course my commitment now was the haven. With Wick House and Bris House it was all getting a bit over the top. I always said that when I sold Wick house I would take the top staff on holiday, on a cruise. Because I've always said, that it's your staff that create the business and it's them that make it all worth while. I have to go very careful how I advertise it. Round about this time I have a manager called Bill Docherty, who is responsible for dishing out extra sheets, pillow cases extra bedding, etc. when it was needed for the different homes. He came into the office one day and said "I keep getting requests for extra pillows and extra sheets and covers from Wick house. What are they doing down there?. I said "It's probably just matron Smith keeping everything top drawer"

"I don't know" he said, "seems a bit odd to me"

I managed to get some people, called the Ergans, who had a nursing home in Clevedon, near weston-Super-Mare, interested. I knew Matron had a day off, so I would take these people round then. The staff just thought I was showing relatives round. They decided to buy it. It was up for sale at one million. I did not get a million, I got £995,000. The deal was done very quickly. I phoned Bill Docherty and said "Bill be down at Wick

House tomorrow morning at 9'clock". "Yes O.K. Why" "I want you meet Mr. and Mrs. Ergan, they will tell you why they are there".

The following morning we meet at Wick House, The Ergans turn up, shake hands, and tell him they have just bought Wick House. They were then introduced to matron and told her that she now worked for them, not Mrs. Baker.

They were there just over a week when they phoned me and said "We've got keys to everything except one cupboard. Do you have a key". I said "yes, I think so, I'll come over". When we opened the cupboard under the stairs there was everything you could imagine. There were beds, mattresses, bedding, everything. Matron Smith was opening her own nursing home. She had bought a property in Northampton and was nearly ready to open.

The Haven was built by WG Grace, the cricketer, and his brother. Apart from being a cricketer, he was also a doctor, and had a surgery in one of the poorest parts of Bristol. He was supposed to charge patients, but was always willing to work with those that could not afford it, without any payment. He. Had a wonderful reputation. When I was there one day the phone went, and it was a lady whos son had been playing on a ouji board, and got himself into quite a bit of trouble. His mother said, "I've been told to come and see you, you will probably be able to help" So I said, "Yes of course". So she brought the boy round. I told Ron to block off the dining room door, and let me work in there quietly, which I did. As I am working, I saw a gentleman come and sit in the chair, a spirit. He said to me that he was this childs great-grandfather, and that his name was Watkins, and that he had worked at the Haven as a groomsman for WG Grace and his brother. They had a stable at the side of the house, they kept two horses. It was just some evidence, that came from spirit, very nice to have it confirmed, if you like.

Also I should have said, when opening the Haven, we had great difficulty with the powers that be. The health and safety and the fire officer, who both had very different ideas of how the rear kitchen should be used. The fire officer wanted a wall down, and a door put in. The health and safety officer did not want that, because he said the small room beside there, which had marble shelves, was a cold room and we would be keeping food stuffs there in the cool and because the fire officer wanted this door, the door could open and we could have germs waft in and get onto the food. And so there is a big argument about who was going to win. In the end I got very uptight and I took both of them out into the outside hall, and said "Look, I don't care which one of you wins, but whichever one it is I need to know, because I do need to have permission to open in just over a weeks time, please sort it". In the end it was the fire officer got his way and the health man backed down. That's how that got completed.

Wick house was very successful, and once again we didn't have enough space. There was always the waiting list, and I have decided that we needed another wing built on. We contacted an architect, who is coming on the Saturday morning to draw plans to do an extension. When he came he started sketching out what he thought he could achieve. He turned to me and said, "I do not understand why you are building on here, because there is another house up the Road, which is far more suitable for another nursing home. It's absolutely fantastic, it has 240 rooms, it has its own ballroom, it's own church. And at the moment its being used for the staff from the hospitals in Bristol. They are working on eight-hour shifts, so there is a turnover every eight hours of staff, and they are using it as accommodation for the nurses". He said "Avon health have now decided to sell, I think you should go and have a look". So I said "how can I get to it". He said "If you can find Iron Maud lane, you should be able to go in the back way, as I understand it at the moment it's all locked up and Barricaded, they've got extra security on, they've got dogs and extra men on. If you go in the back way, you might just be able to have a look". So I got the car and off I went. I am in Iron Maud lane, and find this tiny little lane going up the back. I came to the edge of the perimeter, to what I now know, was a kissing gate, (old fashion word). So I went through and walked up to the reception. Magnificent looking building, absolutely beautiful. When I got to the front door the security men came rushing out, what are you doing here, what you doing here, you should not be here. I said "I'm very very sorry, but I really just want to stand in reception". He said, "We can't do that". I said "Please, just one minute in reception, that's all I need". very reluctantly he said okay, and I went through to reception and stood in the hall way and I took a deep breath. Chan said "It's yours". So I turned round to the security man and said "Don't show anybody else round, I'm going to buy it". He said you are out of your mind," he said, "they are asking millions for it". I said, "Dont worry, I am buying it." So of course I went home, all excited and told Ted that we were going to have another nursing home. Ted being Ted said "Well that does not surprise me at all". He had got quite used to me by then. As always, we would sit and discuss, and he would say "Only if you think it's the right thing to do, I'll take my coat off". Which meant that he was right there behind me, and it's that strength that he gave me, that I needed to go forward, always.

Then of course, there was the big decision, how much we were prepared to pay for it. I said to Ted "I'm going to tell every one I'm going to offer one million for it, and so we offered 1 million. Because I knew if some people knew our offer they would back off, because they couldn't match the price.

It took us from August to the following October to complete the deal. in the meantime, all sorts of people would walk round looking at the potential. I had a wonderful helper called Mrs Skuse, she had been a house mother in Bris house for years. And her and I got on like a house on fire. When people were walking round, she would walk round with them, and she would say, "Oh, my goodness is water coming through this ceiling? They are supposed to have fixed this roof, there's water in this bucket." Then she would go along a bit further, "Oh, my goodness, those window frames are all coming out". She would keep pointing out defects. And people would say "Oh, I had not noticed that". The best piece was when she got down to the very end of the house, which was Dr Fox's end of the house. She would go into the sitting-room, and in the left-hand corner she would pull back the lino, and she'd see dry rot. "Oh, goodness" she would say, "this needs treating, just look, the floors all going this is terrible". People would be horrified what she was pointing out to them.

One day she phoned me up and she said, "Mrs B you'd better get over here quick," she said, "the builders are in the church and they are talking about putting two floors in the church, and turning the church In to flats". I quickly drove over and went in to the church, and there they were with their clip boards and the measuring sticks. Prior to that I had got in touch with Margaret Thatcher, and discovered that Bris house had not been registered as a listed building. Margaret Thatcher had already written to me and helped me with the purchase from Avon Health. When she was aware of the fact that Bris house had not been listed, she sent a minister down. The day the Minister was down he met Mrs Skuse at the door, and she explained the situation. "Oh, my goodness, as from 12 o'clock today, this is a listed building".

I am in the church talking to these builders and have now got the message that Bris house is now listed. They are deciding what they are going to do. I said that "it seems to me, this is a listed building. I don't think you can do all you said". "It is not listed, if it were we would not be here". "Well "I said, "I think you will find it is".

And so we went on for several months. I had by this time written a letter to the agents and said I was offering1 million for Bris house, which had gone into the archives, because they were going to open the sealed envelopes at a certain time. Coming up to October when the bids would be opened, I'm sat upstairs on the Thursday, and I'm talking to Chan, and I'm saying that I'm having trouble raising the million pounds. So he said "Reduce the offer to £ 750,000." So I phoned Chris Brisley, my solicitor, and said "Chris would you please go and get the letter from the estate agents and put this letter in instead." "Mrs. Baker you will lose it" he said. "No I won't lose it" I assured him. I want you to say, due to the fact, Avon Health have taken the gas boilers, they have taken the sheds from the garden, they have taken this that and the other. The interest rates at the bank have gone up, I am now only going to pay £750,000 and so Chris changed the envelopes. And we waited until Friday morning, the day of the sale. Friday morning I am sat down quietly upstairs awaiting the results, and I'm thinking should I have offered more, when my grandfather appeared and sat by the phone, he looked completely solid, and he said "Keep your head down and your powder dry". Which meant I didn't have to do anything.

The next couple of hours was the longest two hours of my life. I made coffee, should I have offered more, should I not? The phone rang and the estate agent said "If you were to offer another £100,00 I'm pretty sure you would get it". I said "I'm not offering another 100,000 pence, forget it". 12 O'clock the agent phoned again, "Mr. and Mrs. Baker, you are now the owners of Brislington House."

When we went over to bris house Avon Health were there again, removing this and removing that. We then proceeded to get the place into some sort of order. Once again Ted and I with our paint brushes, getting ready for our first opening. We actually open in October. There was so much work to do, and my friends who didn't manage to come and pick up a paintbrush, would like to come and have a look. And so they would come. I would have to put the paint brush down, and go show them round, when I get back the paintbrush is hard. I got fed up, so I said to Ted "I've had enough of this, I am not showing anybody else round. I am going to put an add in thr Evening Post. Telling people that we are now the owners of Brislington House, and are going to open it as a nursing home. If any one wishes to come and view the premises, it will be open Sunday afternoon from 12O'clock. There will be tea and cakes in the ball room. Every body welcome." It happens to be armistis day, 11th November. We duly open the house and Ted being Ted, got himself a bucket and made a very large sign, and wrote on it, wife, two children and stately home to support, kindly give generously. So they came and walked round, threw their money in the bucket. And so at the end of the day Teds got this money in the bucket and he said "What should we do with this money?" Its poppy day, so I said "I think the money should go to the public." And of course the British Legion was so thrilled. The first time they had had such a big donation from Brislington.

When we started to do the different units, Ted felt very much a Bristolian, we should name the different units accordingly. And so our first unit to be open, 23 beds, was Brunell. Our very first lady l to move into Brunel, was a lady called Mrs Gray. She moved in to one of the rooms with all sorts of furniture. When she came to the door we are still painting and mopping, so we stood with brushes and mops held up to form a corridor for her to come through. That was our very first client at Bris house. After we'd been open about three months, a very small hospital in Keynsham was closing, and they have to find places for 15 patients. They rang Bris house, "was it possible for us to take 15 patients?" "Of course we could". And so very quickly, all the rooms were ready and presented and we filled Brunel.

<u>Brislington House</u>

We bought the Woodlands,. Because I got the money from Wick house. My brother had seen it advertised in the magazine, homes and Gardens. He phoned me up and said "". Your looking for a house, I think you should go and see this one at Bath. So I went over to bath to see Woodlands. And I was very very impressed with it, it was beautiful. Chandeliers, and all sorts of wonderful things, it was absolutely perfect. S o we decided to buy it.

The man's name was Williams that we bought it from. This was late August, We were in no hurry to move in because I was still with Bris house. And I was going on a cruise and taking the senior staff, with the proceeds from the sale of Wick house. So Mr. Williams said "Oh, so the house is going to be empty, we really should have somebody living in here while your away. Would you like us to remain here for the next few weeks? We can be caretakers until you're ready to move in". "Oh, yes that would be fine", how stupid. Whilst we were a way, they took the chandeliers, they took the billiard table, from the billiard room upstairs, which was a very big room that we later used for our circles.

When we came back from the cruise, we went to visit Michael in hospital. And then went straight over to Bath, to start to move into Woodlands. Now we had already purchased some Chinese furniture, especially a bar that has a marble top, and opens out. Ted had decided that it was going to go up into the billiard room. So the chaps are moving us in, Ted says "the bar has got to go in the billiard room". "Where is the billiard room" they ask. "Up the stairs and round the corner, it's the room with the billiard table in". So they go bounding up stairs, a few minutes later they come running down, they said "There is no billiard table, there's nothing up there." Ted said "What, that was all part of the deal". We then went into the dining room, the most expensive chandeliers, and another chandelier from the hallway had gone. Ted was absolutely furiouse. We rang the solicitor. "No, Mr Baker you don't want to do anything, lets play the white man, we will go after him through solicitors" Ted was absolutely gutted.

Anyway we managed to get the Woodlands up and running, and we were now using it as a healing centre. We were also using it for the Ark, an organisation founded by some top spiritualists, who were using it once a month for demonstrations by trance mediums, and we had some remarkable evenings there, especially one which I will never ever forget, when Harry Edwards came through. If you can imagine, the room is totaly blacked out. My brother, who is a carpenter, made all the window fittings, that blacked out the light completely. This particular seance Ted and I were there, and you have to make sure you have no jewelery on or anything which can interfere with the ectoplasm, in case it goes back into the mediums body, and cause problems. So we sat there, and this particular night, somebody is doing something with my hands. I'm thinking, what are they putting in my hands. A voice said, "It is not Henry, it's Harry, you will understand what it is, when you see what you have got". So at the end of the seance, the lights go on, and I'm very anxious to see what I've got. It was a gold brooch, with the healing hands. Ted got a pair of cufflinks, green Wellington cufflinks. There's a joke about Ted and the cufflinks. Those are the two things that we have from spirit. These are called apports, something you can't deny. Like when you see daffodils with the teardrops on, just been picked from the garden. That is the sort of thing the Ark used to produce at the Woodlands. I will tell you more about that later.

This is the story of Miss Paige, in Bris house. It's about six o'clock in the morning and the emergency bell is ringing. I just could not believe the emergency bell ringing, because Sister Smith was a very competent matron. She would never ever ring me unless it was in dire need. I ran downstairs in my dressing gown. When I got down, she said," you must come quickly to miss paige's room". Miss Paige had been a charge hand at Cadbury's factory. she would shout, day and night, help, help, help. But when you went in, she would say" There's nothing wrong. I didn't call". And as soon as you left the room, she would start again, help, help,

Unfortunately, her room was just off reception, and it could get very wearing, because visitors coming in could hear this lady shouting for help. This particular night, the sister said "Come quickly" so I go along to miss paiges room, and outside the door are two pairs of slippers. A gentleman's pair, and a ladies pair. Matron pushes the door open, and in the bed is the major and Miss Paige. And matron said "What shall we do". I said "well she's not shouting help, if she does then go in".

Another story about Bris house. I am not really used to doing the squeamier side of nursing. One night sister came to me and said" The girls won't get a break tonight, two have not turned up and we are shorthanded". "Well, what's wrong with my hands" I asked. "Oh, will you help out"? "Of course" I said. Later she buzzed me, she said" You're needed down in Doris's room". Doris is a little lady, tiny little soul, and she's in bed and she has pood. And it's in her ears, in her hair, her hands, it's everywhere. I said "Hang on a minute" I went into the bathroom and got some vick, put it on cotton wool, and stuck it up my nose. We then carried Doris, in her sheet, and put her in the bath to clean her up. When we finished, the nurse said" Mrs Baker, I never thought you would do that" I said "I would never ask anyone, to do anything I would not do". I did not tell her that if it had been the other end, and she had been sick, I could not have helped.

It was a Saturday afternoon, and Ted was running ladder hire, I'm running Arches hotel. I am sat down one end of the settee and Ted is sat at the other end. He's saying "if I could pick up those double 18's from Mrs Ayres, I would have enough to supply Avery's. But if they have not finished with those ladders, I'm stuck". And I'm saying "well if I could move the Williamses out of number nine, and put them in where the Reces are, then I could accommodate the people due to come in next Saturday. And all of a sudden I burst out laughing. When are we ever going to have enough of what we need. We never ever have enough, be it ladders, or rooms, whatever.

I used to supply ladders to BAC, usually August bank holiday. Sometimes it would be 10 double 18's for the holiday break. Another customer, was Beezer French at Ashton. They had rung up for two double 18's to go down over the Easter holiday. They had those ladders for 2 1/2 years. I used to send the invoice Everymonth and they used to pay it. One day the accountant phoned and said "I have just discovered we have got two double 18 ladders". "yes" I said, "that is correct" He said "We only wanted them for Easter weekend. somebody put them round the back of the Garrage, and they have been there ever since.

At Bris House, because we had the lovely grounds, we did all sorts of garden entertaining. We would do summer fairs, various things like that, we also used to have the Salvation Army, they would always come on a Sunday morning and sing in the grounds, because if you were in the grounds, the house could hear. We performed weddings in the church there, and when we first started doing weddings we had to get the City Council to allow us to have a recorder there. It was sometimes a conflict of interest because we would want a recorder, maybe three o'clock on a Saturday afternoon, and the Council house would be short of recorders. They only had three recorders for the whole of Bristol. So one day the council house man phoned up and said "Mrs. Baker, it would make life a lot easier for you, and for us, if you allowed some of your staff to become recorders, and then they can witness the weddings and the weddings would be legal, instead of us having to provide recorder". And so we volunteered three people to become recorders, and they went on courses, and passed out with their certificates. And became official recorders. Which made our weddings a lot easier, because we could accommodate whatever time was needed.

One time when we actually did two weddings in the one day, because not only did we have the ballroom for the reception and so on, we also had the basement. And the basement was where Avon health had used it as a disco, so it had a beautiful floor, and so it was possible to have two functions going at same time. Which of course gave us an extra income. Because I was always wanting to do things and the money had to be found to do it.

We were there quite a few years, and I was getting older, getting tired. We had sold The Haven. When I decided to sell the haven, which I sold before I sold Wick House. We put it to auction, and it went up for auction at the Avon Gorge hotel. I think it actually fetched £365,000. Which of corse was useful money to meet the furnishing for Bris House.

As I said, I was getting older, getting tired, and I said to Ted one day, "I think I'm going to sell, I think it's time that we decided to sell". So he said, "If you think so". I phoned an agent in London, and told them, I explain the premises, told them the size, and what have you. And asked them to put Brislington house on their books, this was on the Wednesday. By the Friday, I decided I did not want to sell. I telephoned the agents and asked them to take it off their books. "Oh, th at's a shame, because we've already put out the details to different people". "Tell them that It's Not for sale" I replied.

Sunday Lunchtime Ted and I are having our lunch and the Lady in reception rings the flat, and says "Mrs. Baker, two large Chauffeur Driven Limousines have drawn up outside the front door. And there's all sorts of very smart gentleman got out, and they want to see you". I went down, and he said "I believe that this place is up for sale". "I'm sorry," I said, "It's not for sale". He said, "Supposing It was, what would you want?" I said "four million pounds". He said, "four Million". I said "yes, don't start arguing, that Is the price". "Would you allow us to walk round". So I said, "Hang on a minute, I'll get Matron to walk round with you". And I Went Back Upstairs. About three and a half hours later they're all downstairs, and they Came back into reception and they want to see me. So down I go again, and this man says "My Name Is Dr Hassain, this gentleman Is Dr. Gooday. We are partners with those other doctors, and We want to buy Bris House". I said "very well, it's just a question of raising the money" "I am part of the Egyptian royal family, and when I say I'm going to buy something there is never any question of money." Dr. Gooday Is a little bit different because he's got a different past. But I'm sure, between them, they are going to to buy.

Now this was quite funny, because off they went home. I later heard, that Dr Hassain was a kidney specialist in Harly street, the other doctor was a specialist also. Over the next months, and it went on. I would get a phone call, "Don't listen to Dr Hassain, we are buying it. We are buying it on our own". We are separated from him, you want four million, we will pay four million. We will let you know when we've got the money". A few weeks later I got a phone call from the other doctor, "Don't listen to him, he hasn't got the money, and will never get it. We are buying it." This went on for months. Eventually I got a phone call from Dr Gooday, and he said "Would you come to London one day next week, at your convenience to discuss the final details of the deal". So I said "yes, what day". He told me, and he said "We are meeting at the Ritz Hotel" I asked Ted if he wanted to come, but he said no, take Bill Docherty. We were collected by limosine, all the way up I said to Bill that we were having lunch at the Ritz. Bill said "Are you sure he's not taking you to a Greek Taverna". I said, "No, definately the Ritz". We get to, the Ritz, there is a man on the door bowring and scraping. They were sat in reception, and I think there were about five or six of them. You could cut the air, because it's blue with cigarette smoke.

They wellcomed me, and started discussing this and that, and it's getting nowhere as far as I could see. It was coming up to 1 o'clock, and I said "I think I would like to go and eat, I've not had breakfast." "Oh, yes, we shall go and eat". I got up and walked from reception towards the stairs leading to the restaurant. He came up and took my elbow and ushured me out the back door. We walked down an alleyway, and where did we go? To a Greek Taverna. For the next hour or so we talk all about nothing. Bill Docherty is laughing because he thought that was where we would end up. Eventually he wishes to continue discussions, we need to go back in the Ritz again. And they sit in reception, and the air is blue, and it's getting bluer, because they are smoking and smoking. Eventually it got to four O'clock, I said "I need to get back to Bristol, I have things to do. You will let me know when you finalise the finance, and we will go from there". "Oh yes" he said.

We travelled back to Bristol, and we wait, and we wait and we wait, we think it's sold but we don't know, we think it is. Eventually I got a phone call from Dr Hassain to say "I have finally managed to purchase Brislington house, and I shall be coming down to take over on Friday. I don't want you moving, I want you staying with me, as long as you are there I know this house will be successful. If you don't think your salary is enough, increase what you are taking. keep the staff, keep everything as it is going at the moment. I am coming down with furniture and equipment. And I will bring my own things down". So I told Ted that I'm not the owner of Bris House, but I'm still in charge. The staff don't need to know any different, because it's going on as normal.

Doctor Hassain came down in the night, and takes out my antiques, and my best carpets, and put stuff in that he's bought from some junk shop. Carry, who is the house mother, came to me in tears. "Have you seen what he's done, have you been down and seen it"? "No". It was absolutely disgusting. I think he must have gone to the cheapest possible rubbish dump you could have gone to. He would come down on Friday and then he would go straight to the mosque. He would then come back, go round the house taking any medication that was not being used. He would go to the kitchen, and tell the kitchen staff to order ten dozen eggs that he would be taking them back to London. He wanted the Bakery unit emptied completely. He had an Egyptian princess coming over, and he wanted one room in particular enhanced He. wanted satin sheets, satin bed covers, because he was going to perform a kidney operation on her, in Bris house. She never materialised.

I'm not bothered because I'm still being paid. Then I discovered that to buy Bris house, he had taken 4 million pounds from the Alliance & Leicester building society, his repayments were £8500, a month. He made one payment. he was in there just over 12 months, by which time I said to Ted, "I just can't take any more, I'm moving out". So I moved out and left him to it. He then went bankrupt, in spite of all his "I'm royalty, and you don't need to worry".

The next phone call I got was from Barclays bank, they said "Mrs Baker, you need to get back in there". I said "What with, with peanuts, I've spent the money, spent it". "oh, come off it" they said, "We are prepared to support you, but you have got to get back in, your the only one that can bring it back". I didn't really want to go back, but if I have to, yes I will. "How much can I get it for". "£ 2.6 million, and we will provide it" So back I go. I have to start now to recreate, what he's destroyed. Fortunately I've still got the staff, the top people had stayed through it all.

I decided that I wanted Diane and Michael to come in with me so I had them in the office and said to Michael "I want you to come back in here. I want you to take over the maintainance. You have a carpenter, a plumber, an electrician, I want you sorting out whatever needs sorting." "If you think I'm going to get my hands dirty, you've got another think coming. I will only come back, if I can have an office job and walk round in a suite". "I'm sorry Mike, we are all taking our coats off and we've all got to take a turn at the wheel, including me." I told him. "Di what about you?" I asked. She said "Mum, I've never done anything in business with you before, and I've never had anything to do with any of the nursing homes. But if you want me in then I will come". So it transpired that Di and I are working together. Unfortunately the staff got the hang of it, because they would decide to do things differently. I would go in the morning about 6-30, and I would say to sister Maddox, "why are you doing so and so like this". "Oh, I talked to Mrs Pearce, (Di's married name) yesterday, and she agreed with me. It would be much better if we did it this way", She answered. "Diane, what have you said to matron" I asked. She said, "I havn't said anything to her". I said "she just told me that you agreed so and so". She said "I don't know anything about it mum". Then it would work the other way, they would say that I said so and so, and in fact I hadn't. It was a conflict of interest and I was again getting very, very, uptight.

Diane was coming into her own, and we again have a conflict of interest, because sister Knight, who is down on Fox's unit was wearing a blue overall, and she is not qualified to wear it. But she is such a good nurse. Although she's not got the qualifications on paper, she is more than competent, and I have so much faith in her, I had said, there was no way she was going to be demoted to a green overall. It didn't matter what, there is no way she was going to get demoted. Which is what the staff wanted. I went on holiday, and the day I went the staff went to Diane, and say, "If we don't agree with what they want, they are going to walk". So Diane said, "O.K. walk out". So four of the top staff walked out. I'm on holiday, I don't know anything about this, I'm on a long weekend in Holland. When I came back Diane told me what had happened, and said she had told them to go. She's busy trying to replace these four people, and of course they take me to the tribunal, and of course I lose. That doesn't matter, I still wasn't going to back down, because Mrs Knight was such a good nurse there was no way I was going to walk away. That became quite an issue.

A interesting thing happened one time while we were on holiday in tenerefe. It was Saturday night and we went to one of Teds favourite pubs, called the Bull, for a few drinks. I was beginning to feel uncomfortable during the evening, because there was a chap there kept Looking at me. I was beginning to feel very uncomfortable. It was getting late and we had had a couple of drinks, and I said to Ted "I think it's time we went love" So we got up, and started walking across the square. This fellow came running up behind me and said "excuse me, you are a medium, aren't you"? So I said, "Yes". So he said "My mother came through, in the spiritualist church,. a fortnight ago. And she told me that I was coming to Spain on holiday and I would meet a medium, who would be wearing a blue frock. It would be late at night, and he had to talk to me, because I was going to be able to help him through a particularly bad patch in his life." He was almost suicidal. So he said "Can you help me?", "Look, I've just come out the pub, I've had a couple of brandies, there's no way I can do anything now". "Can I see you tomorrow" he asked. "So sorry, I'm going home tomorrow" "Could I have your telephone number" he asked. "Certainly".

We went home the next day and I thought no more of it. And then I got a phone call from this chap. Who was now back in England, and he explained to me that he was going through a God Almighty court case, where, can I say, blackmailed, into a billion pounds court case. His mother was communicating with me, and telling me what to tell her son. How to answer what was going on. This went on for about 4-5 months, whilst he was going through the court case, with all the top barristers and goodness knows what. But the outcome was that he was exonerated.

Once again the spirit world, have a wonderful way of working things when they see something is going so very badly wrong. That was just another time when spirit intervened, when they want some injustice put right.

We were well settled at The Woodlands, Thursday was our healing day, Tuesday night was a circle night, and I managed to get involved with Ray Bailey, who is a medium, who now works in Spain. And who at the time, came to Bris house. He had quite a shock to discover that we owned Bris house. He said "I have got something very exciting to tell you". He said "There is a new organisation been created called the Ark" and he said that senior spiritualists are involved, and he said that they are wanting to promote transfiguration, and deep trance seances, and all sorts of things to do with the spirit world. So I said "That sounds very exciting Ray. You'd better come over to Bath" He said "Yes, I live in Taunton at the moment". So we arranged to meet at the top of Batley hill, and we drove into the harvesters, car park. He was thinking we were going to eat in the Harvester. I said "no we are not eating there, if you would like to follow me I have somewhere else to show you"

We drove up the drive, and into the woodlands, "Oh, my goodness" he said. I had been out in the day, because I told Ted that we were going to serve Fish that evening. I had been out and bought three extra pieces of fish. Ted said "We dont need three more, there is only him and his wife". It turned out he brought his wife and his lady love, so I did need three extra pieces.

That was our first meeting with Ray Bailey. And of course from then on, he came and sat in circle with us, and we had some wonderful times, at the woodlands. On one occasion, when the circle room had been blacked out completely, and I said "Oh, dear we are going to need some lights", and the guide said "no, no missy, you don't need the lights, we will bring our own lights" That's how it was the first night. They brought a fluorescent tube down from the ceiling. So we sat there open mouthed. Then he said "Just to prove it is no fluke, the next time we will do it the other way, from side to side". It was just to give us proof that it was the spirit world that were finding it. Our experiences with the Ark were quite fascinating because some of the people that came were so knowledgeable, although we had a lot of knowledge, we learnt a lot from them. And it was a very wonderful experience.

THE WOODLANDS
Bathwick Hill, Bath.

I got involved with a chap called Brian Jones who was very money orientated, and he thought that I still had money from Bris house. And he persuaded me to go in with him, in partnership, in a riding school. For £365,000, it was him and his wife, and another couple, who were horsey people, myself and Ted. He was very domineering, and wanted things done his way, although he was only a third member of the party, he wanted everything how he wanted it. Eventually we had to decide that we were opting out. We told him that we wanted our money back, wanted him out, and wanted to be free of it. And so one night, the solicitor phoned up, and said, "Mrs Baker, can you get yourself down to our offices?" he said, "And be prepared to stay all night. Because we've got Brian Jones on the run, it's not going to be easy. We have got barristers and solicitors here on his side. So we have got to line up our side. Can you get down now"? So I telephoned Di and we went into the solicitors in the middle of Bristol.

We were sat in one room and they were sat in another, and there is going backwards and forwards between the two rooms. About one o'clock in the morning, the solicitor came in and said "Have you eaten"? "No, we have not eaten, "we replied. "Would you like some fish and chips" he asked. So he was sent out to get 20 lots of fish and chips, and we sat there, in the very posh offices, eating fish and chips.

Now I've got to tell you, this went on all night, and at six o'clock in the morning, it was finally resolved, and we walked out of there with the keys to the riding school.

Now I don't know which end of a horse to feed. I very soon found out, Di and I went down to open up, seven o'clock, and the staff arrived, because they didn't know any different. We were confronted with the fact that today, was an open day, and they were having dressage and what have you. And they were expecting a lot of people. There was a tiny little restaurant there, that supplied chips and bacon butties. So Diane and I decided the best thing we could do was leave the staff to get on with what they had to do, and we would get on in the kitchen. We started cooking about nine o'clock in the morning, chips 50 p.a bag, I think by the end of the day, we had made £1000, all day cooking chips. One of the things that amused us was a little girl kept coming in, asking for Polo's, and I said to her, "does your mummy know you are eating all these Polo's?" She said, "they are not for me, they are for my pony".

We had two big arenas there, and a stadium, and an outside display area. It was very successful, but too much work, we didn't really stay very long. Eventually it got sold.

We bought 9 houses at The Home Stead in Keynsham. Why we bought the houses is Michael had come down from London and bought one of the houses. Number 4 had been bought by the manager of Bris House, Bill Docherty. Then we got number 20, the only house we did not get was number 22. Number 22 had a man from Essex, who was a planning officer on the council, so he knew all about planning. We were there a while and it was one of those times, when the country was going through a bad spell.

David Wilson had built these houses, but they were not selling. Ted said why don't you purchase the rest of those houses"? "We have talked for a long time about having a healing village" he said," why don't you make an offer, and see if you can do a deal". So we made David Wilson an offer, and we then bought number 9 number 11 and we were supposed to get number 13, but we didn't like that so we called it number 12. Then we got number 15 and 17. And then I proceeded to furnish them all, top of the tree, absolute top of the tree stuff. We intended doing luxury holiday homes, advertising in America. Butler service, and waitress service, limousine service from Heathrow to Keynsham.

Number 17 was a bungalow, and it was kept for Healing. We were healing on a thursday, day and night. So on the Thursday, lots of people would be coming. There were lots of people in wheelchairs.

Mr Thannet, at number 22 found himself very annoyed about this. He wrote to the Bristol Evening Post. Complaining bitterly about what was happening at Homestead. So the reporter went to see him. He said "how would you like it, to see people in wheel chairs, passing in the mornings. Going to the bungalow for healing". The reporter said "I would be very gratefu, I was not one of those people." It gave a lot of publicity. and we got involved with the Bishop of Bristol, who said that we were evil. The people that Mr. Thannet belonged to, were born-again Christians, and so on the Thursday night, after we'd finished healing. They would go round, with witches brooms, sweeping away the evil spirits that we had managed to entice during the day.

Eventually it got so bad, we decided the best thing to do was to close down. It hadn't taken off as we expected it. So we then set our eyes on the woodlands, and concentrated our healing efforts over to Bath, and into the woodlands centre.

At Bris house we had opened Brunel, partly opened Cabot, and were about to open Fox's, and it's late November. And usually in November I've been out and bought Christmas presents for all the patients. It's always been our practice to go and get presents for all the patients so that Christmas morning nobody wakes up without a present to open. Ted was Christmas, and if he could, it would be Christmas all year round, because he thought everybody ought to be happy. They really ought to be in wonderful spirit because Father Christmas was coming.

We had some wonderful Christmasses. One that comes to mind was when we were living in Hamilton road, in Southville, it was two days before Christmas, and a lady told me that her husband had gone off with another lady, and left her with no money and five children. It's going to be a very bleak Christmas, she had no money to buy anything. So Ted and I set about organising things for the Christmas Festival. We approached Mrs Cheshire, who ran a shop at the bottom of the road, and she gave a lovely Christmas cake, beautifully decorated. And then Ted's father entered the race, because he was making leather handbags, so he stayed up all night and made two extra leather handbags for the two girls. Then the lady across the road, Mrs Whitchurch, gave us toys for the younger children, so that seemed to be a good start, then the next day I went round to the butchers, explained the situation to him, and he gave a small Turkey. Then the man who delivers the vegetables door to door, he gave us all the necessary vegetables for the Christmas dinner. Christmas Eve and with Ted in his father Christmas outfit, round we go to, I think it was Bethnell road, in Ashton, and knocked the door, only to find her in floods of tears because she thought that they had nothing for Christmas Day. So you can imagine the joy and laughter in that house.

Another year, when we were in Harbury road, and we had had our Christmas dinner, just picking over the remains of the turkey, and Michael came in and he said "mum I found these people in Brighton road" which was one of the flats which I had, and he said" they've got no money, and no Christmas dinner. Is there something you can do"? So they came in and we managed to reproduce Christmas dinner for a further six people.

Then there was the time we had the Arches hotel. It was christmas eve and the phone rang late at night. It was Social Services, "Mrs Baker, we have a lady and two children, she's been very badly beaten. We are desperate, can you put them up"? which we did of course, and we fed them and watered them, packed them off to bed." Oh my God, what are we going to do, these children are going to wake up in the morning with no presents". My first call was to Redland police station, "Mrs Baker speaking, owner of the Arches hote, l just had a family brought in and there are no toys for the children". "What what do you expect us to do Mrs." I said "I don't know, but could you do something about it". So then I phoned Di, she brought down a few odds and ends. A policeman knocked the owner of a toy shop up in Gloucester road and explained the situation and he gave some toys which the police brought round. But that's not the end. About five O'clock In the morning, the front doorbell rings, and it's the Salvation Army, they have come round with more toys for the children.

Then of course there's the Haven, and Ted was always so keen that all our patients woke up with presents by their beds. He would always dress up as Father Christmas and go round just after midnight and put presents on their beds, ready for the morning.

At Bris house, it was laughter a minute. Christmas Eve he would go down to Broadmead, which is a big shopping centre of Bristol, and he would come back loaded with all sorts of things. "Don't open that, be careful of this". So always it was a late-night before we ever got to bed. Don't be fooled you ever get a good night sleep when Teds around, or Father Christmases. About an hour or so after your in bed, he's knocking on the doors, "Wake up, wake up, he's been, wake up". And so we all had to wake up. He said "Look what I found at the bottom of the stairs, a bottle of whiskey", he said," He must know what I like". Then we have all the drama of opening the presents, which are on the bed. The two children come in, one either side. Then we all had to take turns opening a present.

My biggest embarrassment was that before Christmas I had gone down into Broadmead shopping, and had gone into a ladies shop and tried on a very luxurious winter coat, with a Silver fox fur collar, beautiful. My friend said "that's absolutely you, super, you should buy it". I said Dorothy, I've come to buy Christmas presents, if I've got money left I wll come back, if not, I w'ont". I never thought anything more about it and went home. On Friday night Michael comes in," very sorry mum, I haven't got any wages for you". "What do you mean, you haven't got any wages"? He said, "Collins had an accident on his motorbike and they rang and said he needed the repairs to be done but they wo'nt do it without being paid." he said "He's promised me next week I will have it back". The next thing Diane came in "Ever so sorry mum" she said, "I have not got any wages for you". "What is going here" Isaid." First Michael, now you, what am I supposed to do"? "Well" she said, "Girl at work had an accident and I lent her the money to help her out. You will get it back next week". So I'm shouting and railing, and Ted says "Don't be too hard on them, they were only trying to help people." Unknown to me of course, the two lots of wages had gone to purchases the coat. So Christmas morning we are opening parcels, mother has the big parcel, when I open it I discovered the beautiful coat. I then realised where the two lots of wages had gone. True to their word I did get the wages the next week.

I think now all you need to know, is how we came to be living in Spain. We were at the Woodlands quite a few years, and it was Christmas. And Ted was complaining about the weather, about the government, about the taxes, and when Ted complained, Ted complained. We were having our Christmas dinner, and our accountant was there, Don Hart. He said to Ted "If you're so blasted fed, up why don't you emigrate. They are doing some beautiful properties in Spain. Why don't you go over to have a look". So Ted said "Okay, we're going to Spain". Don Hart said "where in Spain"? "I don't care", said Ted. "Spain, book three flights for the first week in January". So Don booked the three flights. And that's how we came to be living in Spain.

We arrived at Alicante airport in January. And the first person we met was Heiki, who proceeded to take us to Villa Martin. It was late at night, and she took us to a brand-new apartment, the wrappers have not come off the furniture, cups and saucers are still being unwrapped, and it's freezing cold. I said to her "If you think I'm going to stay here, you've got another thought coming. This has not been lived in, it's freezing. I'm not staying here. Find me a decent hotel." So she rang her boss, and he said "Well we don't want to lose these people, put them in the Torre Hoven hotel." So she booked us in for the night. The next morning she came to collect us. I said "Get me out of here, either find us a decent place or I'm getting on a plane back home. This is a doss house, it's a one night stand. There is no way I'm staying in a place like this again". So she then proceeded to ring her boss again. He said "Oh, dear, you've got to find them a decent place". So she then took us to the Parason Hotel, they have separate accommodation in the grounds, each person has like a little house, very comfortable, very nice.

She took us from there, to go on a sightseeing tour, looking for property. I had seen an advert in the paper which said something about Villa Martin and a house that had a stream running through the garden. I thought that sounds interesting, I'd like to see that one. I can't find anything with a stream running through the garden. Then she found a piece of ground at the side of Villa Martin, which she wanted to sell me for one hundred and ninety thousand, which she assured me, that when it got built I would be able to see the sea from. Yes, if I climbed 3 stories to get on the roof. So I told her what she could do with that. She said," Well, I don't really know where else to take you. "There's a road in Puntaprima", she said," it's called Nicholas Debussy Avenue, they are starting to build houses at the top." So she then proceeded to take us there, she stopped on this corner and she said, "There is going to be 19 houses here". It was built like a horse shoe. she said "Yours would be the corner house, the last one in this road". Houses had already been built on the rest of the road. Ted got out of the car and walked onto where is now our kitchen. It was just as if he'd been struck by lightning. "Oh, my God, oh my God, this is it, this is where we have to be". He was going absolutely loopy. I thought, he's lost it, he's flipped. "Come and stand here" he said, "Just stand here". I must admit when I stood there, I could feel the vibes as well.

So we went back down to see the builder, We told him we wanted to buy, and how we wanted the house built. We paid the deposit, and he said youn will have the keys on June 20th. I thought, yes, I bet. We came over twice to check on things and make sure it was as he said it would be. I must admit, every thing was going absolutely perfect. The morning we moved in there were still people running round the house putting things in place. Our furniture arrived and stopped on the adjoining plot, because the kitchen was not quite ready, the removal men made us tea and toast.

The next six months were hilariouse, we did nothing but laugh. We kept saying, we should have done this sooner. We were due to go on holiday to Alaska on the third of August. We moved in on the twenty fifth of June, and I kept saying to Ted, "I think we should cancel Alaska". "Why do you want to cancel", he said. "Money does not grow on trees" I said. "No, no, no" he said, "We are going to Alaska" I'm so glad we did, IT was a wonderful, wonderful trip, and it was our last holiday.

We came back and settled down to being a bit lazy. He was deciding what he was going to do with the garden, how it was going to be laid out. The swimming pool was made, and we settled down to a nice, quiet, ordinary life. Then a lady who ran a spiritualist church at La Siesta, came to see us. She said that she had been to the SNU and they had told her the Bakers had moved to Spain. She wanted to know if we would go over and take the service in her church. So we settled in to serving the church and doing healing at home. The healing was getting more, and more, and I kept saying, "We've got to buy the plot next door, we have always had a place for healing, we desperately need another one, we've got to find the money some where".

In the mean time he said to me "You have always wanted to go to Corfu, but we have never got there. We will buy a boat and I will take you to Corfu" So we went looking at boats. We came back and were looking at the price of boats, and also looking at the plot next door, which was the only one not sold. So I said to Ted, "Its either got to be the boat, or the plot next door". He said "I don't think there is any contest. It has to be the plot next door".

That's how we bought next door and how we started to get the church built.

And then it's coming up to December, and the time when Ted died. It's just before Christmas and I have been saying to every one, what will happen on 3rd December?. I didn't know what it was, but I was really excited about it, I should have known, it was not the 3rd December but the 4th. So I don't think I'm as good a medium as I thought I was. Weeks before I'd been waking up in the morning all excited, terribly excited, I couldn't think what it was. Looking back now I realise that the excitement was that Ted was going to spirit and would be joining his five brothers and sisters, who had all passed very young.

There would be a very big party over there, and that was the excitement I had been picking up on.

Having to ring Diane and tell her the news was very traumatic, and there was the nightmare because at that time everything in Spain shuts down. All the offices are closed. We could not do this, we could not do that. We wanted to get his body back to Bristol, and we had to have a lead lined coffin, they would not take him without one. That was the first hurdle to overcome. Then of course there was all the paperwork. Then we had to wait for a transport plane, (he could not go on a scheduled flight) to fly him back to Heathrow. I was fortunate that a chap we had been friendly with here was a pilot and he was going back so he accompanied me to Heathrow.

I met Di at Heathrow, we then managed to see Teds Coffin put into a transporter, and we got back to Bristol. Then of course there is a nightmare of having to get the lead lining out of the Coffin, because he's going to be cremated and lead does not burn.

I actually took his funeral service. I knew he would not want anybody else taking the service. It took every ounce of my body to do it, but I would do it even if it killed me. We were able to have it in the church at Bris house, because of course, Bris house was still in our family. I stayed with Di through the December and a few weeks into the new year.

I was very anxious to get back to Spain. She was devastated, she wanted me to stay and give up the idea of returning to Spain. I said "no way, I've got things to do. And so we came back. It was very late at night, and I had forgotten the combination of the security system. While we had been away, we'd been in touch with Heiki to get round to sort everything out. And get the combination and the locks changed, everything. Which she did.

We are now here, and it's midnight, and we're trying to break in, which we can't. Sirens going off, and the next minute the police arrived with guns dogs the lot. They are going round the perimeter, going absolutely mad, demanding passports. Now Mike Pearce is with us, and so he gives his passport. They go absolutely bananas, because his name is Pearce, not Baker. So they are going to lock him up. They started marching him out through the door, so I said "Don't worry Mike, we will get you out in the morning". He didn't take too kindly to that. By this time Heiki had arrived and managed to sort everything out, calm things down. And eventually we got to sleep

Diane was absolutely crazy, she thought I was mad. She thought I should give it all up, and go back to England. But there was no way. I went down to Alphonso, the builder, and showed him the plans. I Told him what I wanted. He said" You will have the keys on July 25", and that was when I got the keys.

He was quite a good friend to me. I think he realised the vulnerability of me being on my own. He did all he could for me. I went to Corte Englaise and bought what I thought was sufficient, 50 knives and forks and spoons, plates, etc. Because I thought we would be doing dinners from time to time, but that has not happened.

We brought 20 people over from Bristol, who had sat in circle with us at Woodlands and elsewhere, to take part in the first service. I thought this was wonderful. We had to find accommodation for them, I knocked somebody's door, down by the seafront. When the lady came to the door, she looked so ill. I thought, I know why I knocked this door. She said "I understand you do healing". I said "yes we do, you must come to healing", which she did.

We worked with her for several weeks, but unfortunately, the cancer was so far gone there was very little we could do, but we did manage to make her life more comfortable for her. Her husband is still a friend of the church, and from time to time sends us people that need healing.

I was asked to take an afternoon clairvoyance session at La zenia. When I got there, I did the clairvoyance, and halfway through the afternoon I said to this couple, "You two are healers, you have got to come and see me at the church". They looked at me a bit blank. It turned out to be Russ and Beryl, and they worked in the church as healers for quite a while.

When I was going to Corte Englaise, I met a couple called Carol and Keith, who were strong supporters of the church, and support to me.

I must say the sanctuary has been one of my best moves, and one of the happiest. Because it gives me great pleasure to go over there and work from time to time, and it could not have happened if we had not moved to Spain

Messages from Ted

It ought to be emphasised how clever Ted was. When he was leaving school his headmaster said this boy has got a fantastic brain, and if he does not go to university it will be sacrilege. No way he can afford universities, he was denied the opportunity of having further education. His education came first of all from the spirit, but he also did an open University course, and he was one of the top students.

I should also mention some wonderful messages I've had from him, one of them was when seven trainee mediums were over here from Bournemouth. Tony chaps said "Mrs Baker, I think I've got Mr Baker here, he's telling me that he's building a large house for you overlooking water. And he's been out and bought two chandeliers, what does 2 chandeliers mean? I said "you couldn't have given me a better proof, because every time I bought a house, I bought two chandeliers." Ted had always promised that eventually you will get a house overlooking water because that's how I had grown up.

One night I left the hosepipe running in the garden. It was about nine O'clock at night and I came in tired, got myself into bed, when Ted says "you have not turned the water off" "Don't be stupid" I said, "of course I have"." No you have not". Reluctantly I got out of bed, and there is the hose washing the road.

Again it's coming up to Christmas and I was over the church on Tuesday for clairvoyance evening. Nadine was taking the service and said "I've got Mr Baker here, and he's telling me you must go and get your ring checked". There was nothing wrong with the ring that I could see. On the Thursday morning after giving healing there is a stone missing from the ring. I keep getting the message, the stone is in the house. I can't find it anywhere, Heiki came in and we went over with the vacuum cleaner with a stocking over the end. I shook everything, looked every where, no stone. I took the ring to Mercadona for repair on the saturday. On the Sunday morning, sat there in the lounge and the medium taking the church service came in, and she said. "What's that on the floor" And there was the missing stone. I took it to Mercadona on the Monday and had it refitted. Ted was right, it had been in the house all along.